BASIC RESTAURANT THEORY AND PRACTICE

MICHAEL ANKER
VINAY K BATTA

BASIC RESTAURANT THEORY AND PRACTICE

Longman
Scientific &
Technical

Longman Scientific and Technical
an imprint of
Longman Group UK Limited
Longman House, Burnt Mill, Harlow
Essex CM20 2JE, England
Associated companies throughout the world

First published 1987

British Library Cataloguing in Publication Data

Anker, Michael
    Basic restaurant theory and practice.
    1. Table service
    I. Title   II. Batta, Vinay K.
    642'.6   TX925

ISBN 0-582-41358-3

BSDCS7

Set in Linotron 202 10/12pt Times
Produced by Longman Singapore Publishers (Pte) Ltd.
Printed in Singapore

Dedication

1. To the training given by Strand Hotels Ltd., and the then Westminster Technical Institute, without which this book could never have been written.

1983

2. To the memory of a great friend and colleague, Vinay K. Batta, so sadly taken from us in July 1985. He had so much to give and is sorely missed.

MICHAEL ANKER,
October 1986

CONTENTS

PREFACE

In spite of presentday technology, the service of food in the classic mould of the the 'Restaurant Français' which exists in most hotels of note as well as in individual restaurants of repute has not changed. The classic basic skills must therefore be taught and learnt with enthusiasm in order to produce the desired result for both the customer and the establishment.

The purpose of this book is seen by the authors as fulfilling a need – that of expanding on the practical elements of food service, to which most authors in the past have given scant cover.

Previous works on the subject have omitted the obvious in their covering of the subject matter, and it is our belief that learning of psychomotor skills can be greatly accelerated by teaching the obvious, which is so obscure to the learner.

This book is primarily intended for the practical skills element of the City & Guilds' Food Service Certificate No 707/1, but will be equally applicable to B/TEC Certificate and Diploma courses. The book will also serve as a handbook for those involved in the industry, who train personnel for food service.

The practical elements contained within are couched in objective terms similar to those of the examining bodies, allowing for easy reference. We have taken the approach that in order to perform a task, two elements must be present – skill and knowledge; although no skill can be performed without some knowledge, a major part of the knowledge component assists only in the development of professional competence. In view of this, this knowledge component is analysed into:

must know
should know
could know

so far as is practically possible, in order to give a complete rationale to the skills.

The first part of this book contains fundamental background knowledge on which the skills will be built.

The second part contains the basic skills which are used time and again to perform various food service tasks. These skills must be mastered before attempting to learn the food service tasks which constitute the third part of the book.

In the second and third parts, the emphasis is on the skills element, with the relevant part of the knowledge element.

Our experience in the past has shown that in order to accelerate the acquisition of basic skills, only the 'must know' of the knowledge component need be included in the early stages, so as not to hide the skill in an unnecessary mass of knowledge.

Additional background knowledge related to those skills and tasks has been classified and included in the fourth part.

Although useful for teacher or trainer, this book will be invaluable to the keen 'student' in acquiring the skills on his own.

Throughout the book the authors have endeavoured to reflect the current practices and standards of the industry in general, but wherever there is a possibility of more than one acknowledged variant, every effort has been made to cover it. However, variations must exist and adaptation may occur.

ACKNOWLEDGEMENTS

We wish to acknowledge with gratitude the help of the Principal and Head of Department of Catering Studies at Southgate Technical College for use of facilities needed to produce the photographs taken by the authors.

For constructive comments during the time needed to produce the work we thank M. R. Anker of Stafford Technical College, and G. Shurman of South Downs College.

For other photographs and facilities generously supplied, we are indebted to the following firms and organisations:–
G. N. Burgess & Co. Ltd.; Buttapatta Co. Ltd.; Crest Hotels Ltd.; Hobart Mfg. Co. Ltd.; The London Coffee Information Centre; Moore, Paragon U.K. Ltd.; Arthur Price of England; Sea Containers Services Ltd. (V.S.O-E); Sheldon Cutlery Division of Chinacraft Ltd.; Steelite International p.l.c.; W. M. Still & Co. Ltd.; The Tea Council; Trusthouse Forte Restaurants Division (Café Royal).

We have tried to give all due acknowledgements to any text or photographs, but should any have been omitted, we tender our apologies and suggest that anyone having any claim on any text or other item contact the publishers when their names will be added to the acknowledgement list in any future printing or edition.

Lastly, we acknowledge a debt of deep gratitude to our wives and families for the time spent preparing this work, which would otherwise have been spent in their company.

M. Anker
V. K. Batta

1

THE HOTEL AND CATERING INDUSTRY

FIG. 1.1 Frontispiece

1.1 HISTORY AND DEVELOPMENT OF THE INDUSTRY

Although we now see the hotel and catering industry in fourth
position in the UK industrial league table with regard to the number
of employees and annual turnover, in its present state it is of fairly
recent origin, dating from the introduction of regular mail coaches
in the late eighteenth century, and developing further, with the
advent of railways, and then the motor car, which gave ordinary
man the means to travel more easily than he ever had before.

There had certainly been inns since biblical times, and no doubt
before, and all the eastern religions, at least, enjoin one to
provide food and drink for the traveller as an obligation which has
continued even down to the presentday legal requirements of the
Hotel Proprietor's Act 1956, in the United Kingdom.

The history of the industry is tied up with its etymology in several languages, and some terms come and go in popularity from time to time. The two main roots would appear to be Latin and German, as follows:

LATIN	GERMAN
Hospitale = a place for guests,	Herbergen = to hide or shelter (in)
whence: Hospitality	whence: Auberge (Fr.)
Hospice	Albergo (It.)
Hostel	Inn (Eng.)
Hostelry	
(H)ostler	Gast = Guest
Hôte (both host	(Ger.)
and guest!) (Fr.)	Gasthaus = Inn
Hôtel (Fr.)	
Osteria (It.)	Gastgeber – Innkeeper
	Gastwirtschaft – The Catering or Hospitality Industry

Originally the obligation to care for travellers on the road in predominantly Christian countries was taken up by monastic orders, but in England, after the dissolution of the monasteries, this task was carried out either by the landed gentry, as an obligation, in their manor houses, which were *private*, or by innkeepers, in their houses, which were open to the *public* (hence public houses).

1.2   THE RESTAURANT AND ITS VARIATIONS

The origins of the restaurant are as old as those of inns and hotels, but since the eleventh century have been linked with taverns and ale-houses.

Originally taverns would supply bread and cheese or meat to their guests; later cook-shops were established which took over these tasks, either on their own, or ancillary to bakers, making meat pies etc. These and other cooked meats would be eaten mainly off the premises, but some offered accommodation for those wishing to eat.

By the 1650s the habit in towns and cities of some people of meeting and eating together was commonplace, and on the introduction of the new beverages of tea, coffee and chocolate, these were added to the list of previous victuals on offer. They also provided newspapers to be read, for those who could. In the beginning of the eighteenth century 'ordinaries' had appeared. These were eating places which provided bread, meat and ale daily, and were both generous and cheap.

Originating from the French *se restaurer* (to restore oneself), the word 'restaurant' did not appear until 1765 in Paris, and did not cross the Channel until the middle of the nineteenth century. As the railway companies built large, prestigious hotels, they installed the classic 'French' restaurant with full silver service, which was quite foreign to most English people, but which soon became very popular. When travelling became more commonplace such establishments appeared in smaller towns, and the coaching inns which were then on the wane up-graded their 'ordinaries' into restaurants.

The idea of 'eating out' appealed to the masses, and at this time many changes took place. In 1884 the Aerated Bread Co opened its first tea-shop, followed some ten years later by J Lyons & Co – the fore-runners of two great chains which were to sound the death knell of the taverns and chop-houses.

At first the tea-shops served only teas, then more substantial meals, becoming very popular with women, who could not, at that time, frequent taverns unless escorted. In 1873 the Great Northern Railway Co ran the first restaurant car on its trains between London and Leeds.

Restaurants of all types sprang up, especially in London. In the area of Soho, with its largely French and Italian population, many different types of restaurant and café flourished, and it became the centre of the London catering industry, and the nursery that was to provide most of the staff of the large hotels that were being constructed at the turn of the century.

These hotels all had large palatial restaurants full of brass and marble, with crystal chandeliers using the new electric light and everyone dressed for dinner, and were served from sumptuous à la carte menus.

Many of these hotels had Grill Rooms, which resembled the restaurants, with similar menus, but in which it was not obligatory to dress.

At this time also, with the advent of steel-framed buildings, large rooms could be constructed without the pillars which previously had been necessary and these could be used for large gatherings and banquets, which at this time reached the peak of opulence, and meals of 14 courses were not unknown.

The advent of the First World War in 1914 and the necessary rationing of food led to a reduction in the numbers of courses, both in banqueting and in normal restaurants, and the presentday standard of three or four courses with coffee came into vogue.

This was reduced again during the Second World War and Government restrictions from December 1939 led to menus containing such notices as 'only one main dish allowed', or 'no more than one underlined dish', with a maximum selling price of no more than 5 shillings (25 pence), which lasted through a period of some eight years until 1952, when it was finally lifted. (A surcharge of 2 shillings (10 pence) on the price of 5 shillings was allowed if a live band played music during meals!)

After the lifting of the last of the wartime restrictions conditions gradually returned to those of pre-1939, but as the pace of life had quickened, and also due to the large numbers of foreign troops stationed in Britain, other types of catering operation appeared.

Milk-bars on the pattern of the American drug-stores, with long counters, had appeared during the 1930s and they began to proliferate, followed by a vogue for coffee bars with their Italian 'espresso' machines and juke-boxes in the early 1950s.

The marble and brass of the classic restaurants continued, but in the popular restaurants table linen disappeared, and both tables and walls were covered in Formica or other plastic finishes, and eventually even the waiter and waitress service of the J Lyons & Co's tea-shops and 'Corner Houses' gave way to self-service, on the cafeteria system, before disappearing altogether, although the 'Wimpy' bars started by Lyons as a franchise operation still exist, in competition with the more recent US imports of McDonald's, Burger King, Wendy's etc.

In many hotels, due to the changing eating habits and in an endeavour to counter inflation by not offering a full floor-service, only one classic 'French' restaurant-type operation may be available, open only during the lunch and dinner periods. A 'coffee-shop' type operation usually open for up to 18 hours per day will supplement this, in airport hotels open for 24 hours, and these will be supplemented by the provision of kettles and individual portions of instant coffee, 'non-dairy whitener', sugar, tea-bags, and even cereals, rolls and jam for a 'do-it-yourself' morning beverage and/or continental breakfast. A modern coffee shop is shown in Figure 1.2.

Bistro-type individual restaurants have become very popular; so also have other ethnic-based operations with many different types of catering, such as Italian, Indian, Pakistani, Bengali, Turkish,

FIG. 1.2 Coffee Shop – Crest Hotel, Eastleigh

Greek, Chinese and many others, offering both table service and 'take-away'.

Although not exactly within the scope of this book, mention must be made of other types of catering operations, such as in-store catering found in departmental stores, and other non-commercial operations such as hospital, services and prison catering, and usually subsidised operations such as industrial canteens, where service styles range from self-service for works staff to full silver service for directors' dining-rooms.

Shipboard catering is identical with that found in first-class hotels, but apart from the service on 'Concorde', most airline catering is composed of pre-prepared trays, where a whole meal is served to passengers at once.

Railway catering also varies from cafeteria service to waiter service, with trolley sales down the length of trains for snacks, drinks etc. Figure 1.3 shows the opulent interior of one of the 'Orient Express' Pullman cars.

1.3 NECESSARY FEATURES FOR A RESTAURANT

A conscious choice must be made by management about the type of restaurant that they wish to operate.

FIG. 1.3 Pullman car interior (Venice–Simplon–Orient Express)

Many options are open to them, and all must be considered:
1. Is the restaurant to be operated as self-service, or with waiting staff?
2. If with waiting staff, will the food be served on plates direct from the kitchen, or will the waiters employ 'silver service'?
3. What of the restaurant itself? Will it be in the classic or modern style, rustic or ultra-modern?
4. Will table linen be used, or plastic or polished wood tables?
5. How large will it be? How many customers are envisaged?

No matter how the above questions are answered, toilet and cloakroom facilities must be provided, and probably, if the restaurant is to be in the classic style where guests are not in a hurry, there must be a comfortable waiting area, perhaps with a bar where intending guests will wait for a table to become available, and also possibly where they can relax over coffee after the meal, if this is not served in the restaurant proper.

Décor is also most important in conveying the image to be projected, as are good climatic conditions for the diners, neither too hot nor too cold, with no draughts or kitchen odours allowed to enter the dining-room, and sufficient ventilation to remove tobacco

FIG. 1.4 Dining-room – Plough & Harrow (Crest Hotels)

smoke, if smoking is to be permitted. Figure 1.4 shows a modern, small hotel restaurant.

To sum up, the restaurant, of whatever type, must attract the type of customer for which it was planned and give the necessary air of comfort, aided perhaps by the judicious use of flower arrangements, etc.

Tables must be large enough to permit sufficient tableware to be put on them for the number of diners envisaged at each; chairs must be comfortably upholstered for de luxe restaurants, but be not quite so comfortable for popular restaurants, and only rudimentary for the majority of seating in fast-food restaurants where diners are positively not encouraged to sit over a meal, but to move out after eating, to make way for other customers.

Carpets, if fitted, should be of best quality, to ensure long use, and there should be sufficient space between seated guests to permit the free passage of waiters between them, together with trolleys, etc, without banging into the backs of chairs, or catching tables.

1.4 RESTAURANT ANCILLARIES AND OTHER CONNECTED DEPARTMENTS

The restaurant manager will usually have control over the following ancillaries: Still room; Silver store and Plate room; China store (buffer); Glass store (buffer); Restaurant pantry; Restaurant linen store; Cutlery and Crockery washing-up area.

In a hotel the restaurant will have contact, to a greater or lesser degree, with the following departments as necessary, some on a daily basis, and some only on a 'when needed' basis: Dispense bar and cellar; Cashier's department; Linen room; Dry goods store; Control Office; Stewarding department; Housekeeping Department; Maintenance and Engineering departments.

The hotplate area will come under the direct control of the Head Chef.

The ancillaries as listed above must be situated outside the restaurant proper in a suitable position to allow for a logical work-

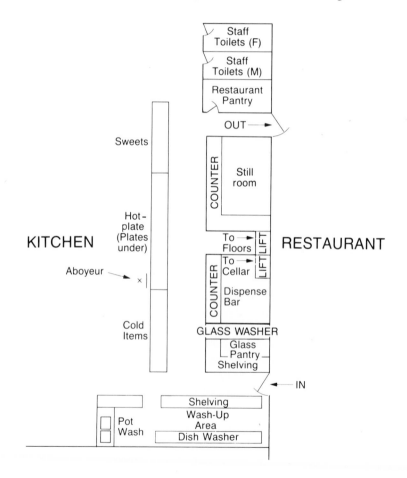

FIG. 1.5 Plan of typical restaurant service area

flow, permitting waiters to deposit soiled items for washing-up before collecting cold items from the kitchen followed by hot, so that the heat from hot food is not lost while it is in the service area.

A typical lay-out of a restaurant service area is shown in Figure 1.5.

1.4.1 STILL ROOM

The name 'still room' originates from a room in which distilling was carried out in a large house, and which later became the house-keeper's storeroom. It is not named, as is erroneously believed, after the well-known British manufactures of café-sets and water boilers, Messrs William Still & Sons Ltd of Hastings, two of whose products are shown in Figures 1.6(a) and 1.6(b).

Its purpose in a restaurant is as a kitchen subsidiary, providing and producing all non-alcoholic drinks, other than squashes and cordials, such as tea, coffee, cocoa, chocolate, proprietary beef drinks, tisanes (herbal teas) and milk (hot and cold).

It is also the area in which are prepared supplies of butter, bread, toasted items, rolls and breakfast boiled eggs. In hotels which offer an afternoon tea service in the lounge, toasted tea-cakes, buns, crumpets, etc will be prepared in the still-room – pastries and sandwiches coming from the pastry section of the kitchen and larder respectively.

Utensils necessary for the service of the above, teapots, coffee pots, milk and hot-water jugs, etc will also be stored in the still room.

Depending on the system used, either a hot-water boiler or a combination café-set, with coffee percolator and coffee and milk holders, together with a steam injector, will be situated in the still room, together with a butter-pat machine, a refrigerator, and in a restaurant where a large breakfast trade can be expected, a toaster and salamander, as well as a bread-slicing and buttering machine, a sink with draining-board and an egg boiler. If used, stocks of individually wrapped butter portions, tea-bags, and individual portions of jams, marmalades, etc, will also be stored there. A typical arrangement is illustrated in Figure 1.7.

1.4.2 SILVER STORE AND PLATE-ROOM

Depending on the type of operation of an establishment, both table silver and flat-ware may be kept in a locked store due to its inherent value, and only issued on demand, on a daily basis, against a signed

STILL'S
RAPIDE GAS
HEATED
BOILER
(BRG 200)
WITH
SB4/CM
COFFEE
MACHINE
AND MU2 MILK
URN ATTACHMENTS.

FIG. 1.6(a) Typical café-set and boiler (front removed to show boiler (W M Still & Sons Ltd))

FIG. 1.6(b) Latest type of 'Electromatic Mk II' café-set (W M Still & Sons Ltd)

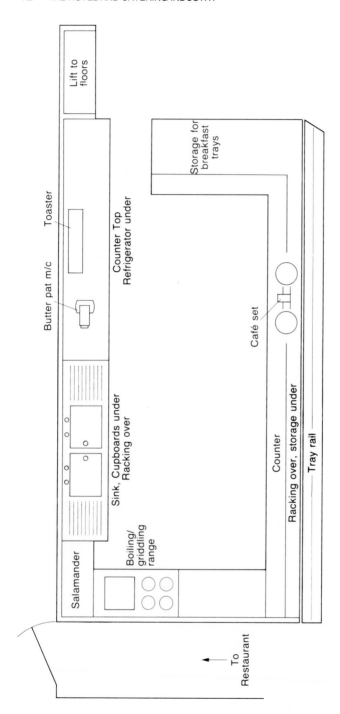

FIG. 1.7 Plan of typical still-room

requisition. In other places the whole of the table silver will be kept in the restaurant or restaurant pantry (see section 1.4.5) with flat-ware being stored in the kitchen area.

All silverware must be kept highly polished and in good order, and in smaller restaurants the table silver will be polished by the restaurant staff on a weekly rota basis, while in larger establishments a staff of platemen/women will perform this task in the plate-room.

This room will be equipped with a burnishing machine for cleaning small items like cutlery and hollow-ware such as tea and coffee pots etc. It consists of a rubber-lined drum which rotates and is half filled with ball-bearings. The items to be cleaned are put into the drum, which is then topped up with a soap and water solution, the lid is locked down and the motor turned on. The rotation and consequent friction gives a high polish to the articles.

The room will usually contain a baize-covered table for use when cleaning large flat-ware items, and if the staff is qualified, they will also carry out minor repairs, straightening, etc.

Flat-ware or small items may also be cleaned by other methods, as follows:

'Polivit Plate'.   A pierced aluminium plate which must be placed with the articles to be cleaned in a metal vessel, preferably heated by gas, electricity, or steam, together with a strong solution of washing soda (sodium carbonate), and the resultant chemical action will remove tarnish.

'Silver Dip'.   A proprietary solution, which will remove tarnish from silver or silver-plated items if dipped in it. This is very useful to remove the black tarnish from fork prongs after use with certain foodstuffs, such as eggs, between the regular cleaning periods.

'Plate Powder'.   A proprietary powder, or common whitening mixed with methylated spirits, is rubbed onto silver or plated items with a rag and allowed to dry, after which it is rubbed off with a soft cloth, and then buffed up with a soft brush, especially if the items are patterned or engraved.

'Silvo'.   A proprietary product similar to a solution of Plate Powder. The above notes apply.

'Duraglit'.   An impregnated wadding, used in a similar fashion to 'Silvo'.

Whichever method is used all items must be thoroughly washed after cleaning before re-use.

For stainless-steel cutlery and flat-ware the only treatment necessary to keep it in good order is washing in a good detergent solution and final drying with a lint-free cloth, although in the interests of hygiene it is better to use a properly-maintained dish-washing machine with the correct washing product, since they are perfectly capable of handling all cutlery, either silver-plated or stainless, provided that they do not have bone or plastic handles.

1.4.3   CHINA STORE (BUFFER)

For a large restaurant a buffer store of china may be kept to cover extra requirements for use when necessary and to supplement the stocks carried either in the restaurant itself, the wash-up area and/or the hotplate.

Major back-up stocks would be kept in a large store at or near the goods-receiving area and would be under the responsibility of the storeman or buying department.

The buffer store could be a small store-room or cupboard, and china should be kept on shelves made of stout wooden slats, or on metal racking such as Dexion or other proprietary system, depending on the volumes of stocks kept.

Heavy items, such as joint plates, platters etc, should be stored at low levels because of the weight involved, with smaller items such as cups, saucers, etc, at higher levels.

When stacking, great care must be taken that stacks are stable and will not topple, and not stacked so high as to cause fracture or cracking of those items at the bottom of the stacks.

1.4.4   GLASS STORE (BUFFER)

The notes above on storage of china apply also to the glass store, except that glasses should be stored in the boxes in which they were delivered, or arranged in specially constructed glass trays that can be purchased for the purpose.

1.4.5   RESTAURANT PANTRY

The size of this may vary from a corridor between still room and restaurant to a room which may contain the still room itself, together with the wash-up area, the glass pantry and wash-up, the dispense bar, hot storage for plates etc, and if the kitchen is not on the same level, a food lift in direct contact with the kitchen. There will also be cupboards for cruets and condiments, cutlery and other restaurant equipment not kept in the 'room'. A dirty-linen box may also be situated here to receive soiled linen.

A staff of pantry-men or women will be employed to assist the waiting staff and will be responsible for the cleanliness of the area.

The layout must be logical to avoid criss-crossing of staff in the area and possible accidents. A typical layout is shown below and is arranged so that waiters will deposit used glasses, plates, crockery etc, before collecting new orders, and these new orders will be collected in the order of drinks, then cold food, followed by hot, in order that hot food does not become cold while other items are collected. A typical arrangement is shown in Figure 1.8.

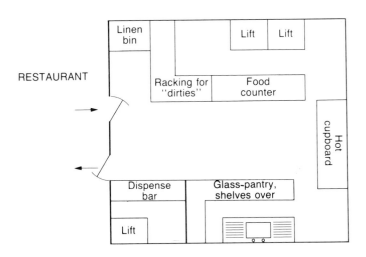

FIG. 1.8 Plan of typical restaurant pantry

1.4.6   RESTAURANT LINEN STORE

If the restaurant is part of a hotel, it will only carry sufficient stocks of linen to cover at most one whole day, and at least sufficient for the next meal service.

Table cloths, slip cloths, waiters' cloths, serviettes, together with glass cloths, sideboard cloths and dusters would normally be held, and 'dirties' exchanged with the main linen room on a 'one-for-one' basis, i.e. a clean item issued for each soiled one returned.

The initial stock level to be carried in the restaurant store would be decided upon by management depending on the usage established over a period.

The store could be either a small room or large cupboard, equipped with paper-lined wooden slatted shelves. All stocks should be kept covered with clean white paper to exclude dust and stocks must always be rotated as table 'linen' deteriorates from standing too long unused.

1.4.7   CUTLERY AND WASHING-UP AREA

This area will always be found nearest to the 'out' door of the restaurant to enable waiting staff to unload their trays of 'dirties' before proceeding to the hotplate area. Size and type of dishwasher used will depend on the average number of covers served in the restaurant and the size of stocks of crockery and cutlery maintained in order to ensure no delays to waiting staff. A large volume throughput dishwasher is shown in Figure 1.9(a) with the various processes shown in Figure 1.9(b).

Tabling to receive 'dirties', or a 'carousel' should be of an adequate size to receive the amounts of crockery and cutlery likely

FIG. 1.9(a) Latest 'Flight' dishwashing installation (Hobart Mfg Co Ltd)

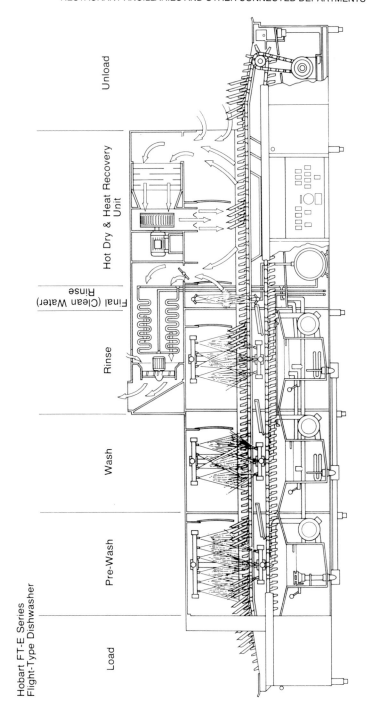

Hobart FT-E Series
Flight-Type Dishwasher

Load | Pre-Wash | Wash | Rinse | Final (Clean Water) Rinse | Hot Dry & Heat Recovery Unit | Unload

FIG. 1.9(b) Features of the 'Flight' dishwasher

to come in at any one time to avoid building of dangerous 'towers'. Adequate staff must also be employed to clear and stack both dirty and clean ware in order to give a good service to all waiting staff.

Glasses may also be washed in a dish-washer, but this practice is not to be recommended in view of the possibility of breakage, and, unless a water-softener is employed, many dishwashing machines leave water spots on glasses which 'bake-on' due to the heat of the rinse water and the thin walls of the glasses.

The best method of washing glasses is to use a glass-washing machine of one sort or another, depending on amount of throughput, and storing glasses in purpose-made trays according to the size of the glasses, thus avoiding undue handling and possible breakage.

Proper racking should be installed to take plastic storage trays used for both crockery, glassware and cutlery, so that waiting staff can always find items needed, without hunting for them.

Care must be taken that water leaks etc in this area are avoided in order that waiting and other staff do not slip on wet or greasy floors.

1.4.8   DISPENSE BAR AND CELLAR

The dispense bar exists to dispense waiting staff only with their requirements of alcoholic beverages, mineral waters and all those drinks not served from the still room or kept in the restaurant on a liqueur trolley.

Depending on the layout of the building, the dispense bar may form part of the cellar if it is on the same floor level. If not, it is best connected with the cellar by a service lift, large enough to carry bottle crates, kegs and gas cylinders etc.

If separated wholly from the cellar it should carry sufficient stocks of all items on the wine list to cover either one meal service or a whole day, being re-stocked during the morning or during the afternoon.

The dispense bar should contain wine racks for red wines, cooled cabinets for white wines, cooled slab stores for bottled beers and minerals, an ice-making machine, bottle opener and 'optic' measures for normal spirit lines stocked, together with a sink and draining-board.

All issues made will be made against waiters' checks only, no cash being taken.

1.4.9   CASHIER'S DEPARTMENT

Restaurant contact with the cashier's department will depend, in the main, on the system of billing and accounting used.

Most restaurants will employ a cashier who will prepare diners' bills from waiters' check copies supplied, using the 'continental' or triplicate checking system. Others may use a 'café' type of system, where the diner pays the waiter, who makes out his own bills. Still other restaurants will have bills made out by the head waiter (refer to Section 4.4).

In all cases, *all* bills must be accounted for and summary or analysis sheets made out to account for the business done during the meal or day in question, which must be paid into the main cashier's office (in the case of a hotel), or to the manager, according to house custom.

Recently, much has been made of computerised systems of both billing and accounting, and many hotels operate a system which can report a restaurant diner's bill straight onto his hotel bill.

1.4.10   LINEN ROOM

Mention has been made of the linen room in section 1.4.6 and the maintenance of linen supplies in the context of a hotel will be the full responsibility of this department.

In the case of a free-standing restaurant, management will have decided whether to maintain its own stocks will all the labour and capital costs involved in replacing, sorting, and accounting for linen, repairs, etc, or whether to use a contract linen-hire firm, where linen is sent on a regular basis and replaced once a week or more, depending on usage.

1.4.11   DRY GOODS STORE

Restaurant contact with the dry goods store is normally restricted to drawing supplies of salt, pepper, mustard, sugar, bottled sauces, cleaning materials and paper-ware, such as doilys, paper serviettes (if used), toothpicks, stationery items, etc.

All items must be subject of a signed requisition, and orders for items not normally stocked must be countersigned by an authorised person.

1.4.12   CONTROL OFFICE

The contact between the restaurant and the control office is indirect, normally being made via the restaurant cashier and the control boxes containing checks received in the kitchen, dispense bar, still-room, etc.

The control office's function in this respect is to ensure that all items issued are charged for on diners' bills, or are authorised by a responsible person (head waiter or manager) for free issue, e.g. in case of accident or customer complaint etc.

Another important function carried out by the control office is to report on any fraudulent practices discovered in the course of the control (see also Sections 2.2.12 and 3.2.2.12).

1.4.13   STEWARDING DEPARTMENT

This department is concerned with 'behind-the-scenes' cleaning of kitchen and service areas, and will have very little contact with the restaurant.

1.4.14   BUYING DEPARTMENT

The buying department will only be concerned with the restaurant for the purchasing of new equipment, furniture, cutlery and crockery, or soft furnishings such as curtains, carpets or with printing and art-work for menus.

Decisions for the purchase of any of the above items would normally be made by the restaurant manager in collaboration with the proprietor or general manager together with the purchasing manager. The housekeeper, marketing and sales managers, or food and beverage manager may also be involved, depending on the way that the restaurant is organised, or on the the matter under consideration.

1.4.15   HOUSEKEEPING DEPARTMENT

Contact with the housekeeping department in hotel restaurants is normally restricted to cleaning of soft furnishings, curtains, drapes and carpets unless contract (night) cleaners are employed. Normal day-to-day cleaning operations are usually carried out by waiting staff.

1.4.16 MAINTENANCE AND ENGINEERING DEPARTMENT

This department would normally be concerned only with repairs to the building fabric, or other fixed equipment, such as air-conditioning, ventilating and heating. In a large hotel, 'in-house' staff would be used also, for carpet repairs, french polishing and the like, but in a smaller establishment, outside contractors would be used, or a 'handyman' employed.

1.5   TYPES AND STYLES OF SERVICE

There is a whole range of styles of service used in catering operations.

Some types will overlap and some operations will use one type perhaps for breakfast in a restaurant and another for lunch and dinner served in the same room.

They can generally be divided into two main areas, as follows: Popular catering, Fast-food operations; Restaurant-type service.

1.5.1   POPULAR CATERING

The main types of service found in this kind of operation are as follows.

Take-away
Where a customer approaches a counter and orders from a menu visible during the time he is waiting to be served. Food is intended to be eaten away from the premises and is packed into insulated special containers to keep it hot.

Self-service
Often found in mass catering situations such as department stores, industrial and institutional catering. A customer will take a tray and choose his meal from heated or refrigerated display counters having a tray rail in front. All main-course items are pre-plated, as are any that are 'wet' or 'sticky' and do not lend themselves to being film-wrapped such as sandwiches, biscuits etc.

The normal arrangement of such a counter is that of the customary order of service of a meal, but with the cold items before hot, and hot beverages at the end of the counter-run, just before the cash point. Cutlery and sundries, such as condiments, if not

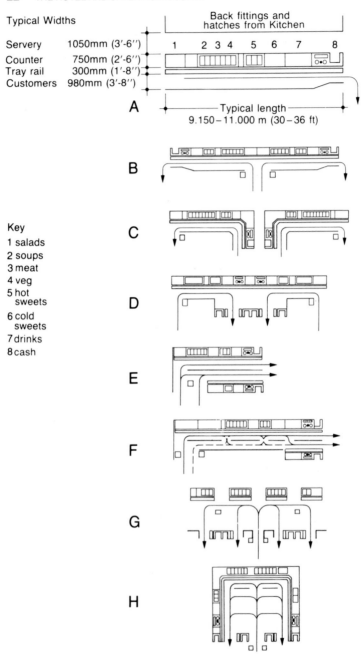

Typical Widths

Back fittings and hatches from Kitchen

Servery	1050mm (3'-6'')
Counter	750mm (2'-6'')
Tray rail	300mm (1'-8'')
Customers	980mm (3'-8'')

A — Typical length —
9.150 – 11.000 m (30 – 36 ft)

B

Key
1 salads
2 soups
3 meat
4 veg
5 hot sweets
6 cold sweets
7 drinks
8 cash

C

D

E

F

G

H

FIG. 1.10 Diagrams of counter-service formats: 1. Single-line counter; 2. Divergent counters; 3. Convergent counters; 4. Convergent counters (alternative); 5. Parallel flow; 6. Parallel flow (with by-passes); 7. Free-flow counters; 8. Perimeter counters

placed on tables will be situated after the cash point, and to one side, in order to avoid crowding.

Clearing of used items in a self-service restaurant can take one of two forms; either customers will take trays to their tables, eat from the tray and return the tray complete with plates etc to a tray-rack, or clearers will be employed to clear used items from tables.

Assisted self-service

Mainly as above, but servers are stationed behind the counter-run to serve main-course items, sweets, etc onto plates for customers. This type of service is not quite so fast as pure self-service, and in situations where large numbers are expected to pass through in a short space of time, various types of counter configurations are used, as shown in Figure 1.10.

The above types of service are also known as cafeteria service or counter service, and both size and configuration will depend on numbers of meals to be served, and the type of menu involved.

Fuller details of these can be found in *Food Service Operations* by P. Jones (Holt, Rinehart & Winston) 1983.

1.5.2 RESTAURANT-TYPE SERVICE

By this one understands a meal served to the customer by a waiter or waitress, the manner of which will depend on the style or type of restaurant, the menu involved and the price to be paid. It may vary from the simple to the complex and each of the main types has its own name and although each is distinct, some establishments will offer a mixture of types.

Plate service

All dishes are prepared and plated complete in the kitchen according to the order given to the waiter by the customer.

Plates/Silver service

The meat/fish content of the dish will be plated in the kitchen, with the potatoes and vegetables served into silver or china dishes for service onto the plate at the table by the waiter/ess.

Full Silver service

All food is prepared in the kitchen and dressed on either silver flats or dishes which are taken by the waiter into the restaurant with hot or cold plates as appropriate and served onto them at the table by the waiter using a spoon and fork at the left side of the guest, unless lack of space precludes this.

There is, with this type of service, some confusion over names. In England the full silver service described above is often called 'French' service, while on the Continent it is usually (and more properly) referred to as 'English' service, for the following reasons: Historically 'French' service or Service à la Française was used in upper-class domestic situations in France, where the waiter would approach the left side of the guest carrying a 'flat' on his left hand on which would be placed a service spoon and fork for the guest to help himself to the food onto a plate previously placed before him. Several disadvantages to this method of service are lack of speed, destroying the display created in the kitchen, lack of portion control, and guests leaving the less-desirable portions to the last to be served.

Full silver service is more properly called English service because it developed from the butler service where the head of the household would carve the joint onto plates, which would be passed to the guests, who would then be served with vegetables, etc, by the butler.

Family service

A similar type of service still exists in boarding houses and hostels, and is generally known as family service. Here the main course can either be served by the waiter, or placed on the table on a plate warmer for the guests to help themselves. Vegetables will be served in the same manner. In Switzerland, even in first-class restaurants, plate-warmers are used, with waiters serving only a token amount of the main course, and leaving guests to help themselves to the remainder.

Russian service

(Service à la Russe) The present-day version of Russian service is that in which a guéridon (side-table) is used, with the waiter who will prepare the dish for service to the guests in front of them instead of at the sideboard. This preparation may involve carving, filleting or flaring, or even the preparation of special sauces.

The name 'Russian' derives from the type of service which originated in early nineteenth-century Russia where landowners wanted hot meals, rather than the situation in French eighteenth century service where all dishes were placed on the table before the guests arrived, the dishes being highly decorated. The Russian system allowed smaller joints and dishes which were carved or prepared for service by the waiters at each table, usually for about 10 people.

The closest type of service to the original Russian type is seen when a guéridon (lit. a small wheeled side-table) is used. The service employed now is more usually a mixture of Russian and English, where the dish is prepared and then dished to be 'silver-served' to the guests.

Banquet service
The type of service used will depend on two main factors, menu chosen and price paid. A silver service banquet will require more staff to serve and thus cost more, whereas a plated meal will be cheaper. A middle way however can be adopted with a hybrid type of service, using plated meats and placing vegetables on the tables for guests to help themselves. Alternatively, silver-serving of the meat or fish will be done, and vegetables placed on the table for guests to help themselves.

Other types of buffet service
Other hybrid types of service are used for breakfasts where beverages, toast etc, are served to guests who then go to a buffet table to choose cereals and hot dishes. Clearing of tables in this case will be done by the waiting staff.

A similar type of arrangement is used in carving restaurants where all items except main course will be served at table, but guests will proceed to the counter for their main course, either carving themselves or being helped by carvers serving from behind the counter.

For function catering, a buffet-type of service is often used, being sparing of staff and allowing guests to choose only those items that they want. Dishes will be artistically dressed in the kitchen. Care must be taken to replace the dishes as they progressively get depleted. The appearance of a half-empty buffet table or dish is not very appetizing.

A small modern function room is shown in Figure 1.11.

Note: In restaurants where 'nouvelle cuisine' is practised dishes are often plated, because the decoration forms an integral part of the dish which would be destroyed if transferred from a flat to the plate by the waiter.

Call-order service
This type of service can exist in several types of catering outlets such

FIG. 1.11 A modern banqueting suite – Plough & Harrow (Crest Hotel)

as industrial, transport cafés and steak-houses. It consists of the normal service counter serving several pre-prepared menu items which will store well, or are cold, and for those items which must be prepared to order, such as grills, fried eggs and griddled items, waiters' requirements are called out to the operatives situated at the back of the service area, who will prepare them on demand.

Note: For a fuller description of all types of service see: J Fuller *Modern Restaurant Service* (Hutchinson) 1983.

1.6   THE RESTAURANT STAFF

Although present-day costs make the employment of unnecessary staff a luxury, most restaurant staffing is based on the classical

French *'Brigade de Restaurant'*, with very few establishments being able to afford to run with the full complement.

The classical system was organised on a strict hierarchy controlled by the Restaurant Manager (*Gérant* or *Directeur de Restaurant*). He would be assisted by an assistant manager *sous-gérant* or First Head Waiter (*Premier Maître d'Hôtel*) who would

**Large Hotel Restaurant
Typical French Brigade**

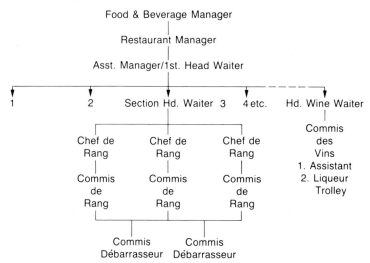

+ Commis on Hors d'oeuvre Trolley
        & Sweet Trolley
Restaurant Cashier

Typical small restaurant

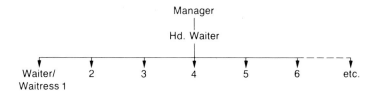

FIG. 1.12 Staff structure charts

deputise for him on days off, holidays or sickness. Figure 1.12 shows the relationship between the various members of staff.

The service in the restaurant would be carried out as follows:

The Section Head Waiter (*Maître d'Hôtel de Carré*) will be responsible for supervising a section (*carré*) of the restaurant, usually three stations (about 15–25 tables). Each section head waiter will also normally have a specific separate duty during the preparation (*mise en place*) period, such as the responsibility for linen, china, silver, stationery or the tips pool (*tronc*). Table reservations and staff rotas are usually the responsibility of the first head waiter or the assistant manager.

Each 20–36 covers would be designated as a station (*rang*) which would be run by a station waiter (*chef de rang*) who will take orders from diners and serve them. He will be asssisted by an assistant station waiter (*commis de rang*) who will not normally serve, but be responsible for taking checks to the kitchen and collecting the food ordered.

Every one or two stations, depending on the establishment, will have a clearer (*commis débarrasseur*) or bus-boy (US) who will be responsible for keeping the sideboards clear of used dishes and plates. They do not approach the table, but will 'use their eyes and ears' and learn procedures from their *chef de rang* and from the *commis de rang*. After some time they may be promoted to the hors d'oeuvre trolley or the sweet trolley (*commis de voiture*) when they will serve diners for the first time.

Wines and other alcoholic beverages, together with cigars and cigarettes, will normally be served by the Wine Waiter (*Sommelier*) who will be assisted by one or more assistants (*Commis des Vins*). The assistants will help serve drinks, and also serve from a liqueur trolley, if used.

Apart from the actual service staff there will normally be a cashier. A recent trend imported from the USA is to have a 'hostess' or 'greeter' who will take over some of the tasks previously carried out by the Reception Head Waiter of checking diners' bookings, seating them and presenting menus, handing the diners over to the *chef de rang*.

It cannot be stressed too strongly that only a large, very high-class restaurant would be able to carry a staff as large as that outlined above, and smaller establishments will have a much less stratified structure, such as a head-waiter and a team of waitresses, the actual number depending on the type and quality of the service offered.

UNIFORM

In the classic restaurant the uniforms for male waiting staff followed the traditions of the Edwardian gentleman, as follows:

Restaurant manager. (Lunch) – Black morning-coat and waistcoat and grey striped trousers, with white shirt and silver tie. In a less formal situation a black jacket would be substituted for the morning-coat.

> (Dinner) – Full evening-dress (tails) with white waistcoat, wing collar and white bow tie. (More informally, a dinner-suit with silk revers (tuxedo US).

Headwaiters. (Lunch) – Black tail-coat, trousers, waistcoat and bow tie, with waistcoat changed to white for dinner.

Station waiters. Black tail-coat, trousers, waistcoat and white bow tie at all times.

Assistant waiters. Traditionally black trousers, white bow tie, white or black short jacket and long white apron.

Wine waiter. As head-waiter with either lapel badge (bunch of grapes), or key or *'tastevin'* on a neck-chain, and in some establishments a short black jacket and green baize apron with badge or other items, as above.

Note: Although the traditional uniform is given above, it is always difficult to keep clean, and with present legislation regarding both hygiene and employers' supply of protective clothing, it is more common for establishments to specify and supply a much simpler type of washable or cleanable type of wear for all service staff, both male and female alike. Colours may now be linked to decor rather than sticking rigidly to black as previously.

2

SKILLS NEEDED

2.1 SOCIAL SKILLS

The profession of Food Service is a skilled profession. Skilled food-service personnel have always taken pride in their profession and such personnel are appreciated and respected by discerning diners.

Because waiters are continually in contact with the diners during the course of carrying out their duties, social skills play a vital role in their jobs.

A waiter needs to develop certain personal qualities and cultivate hygienic and socially acceptable habits if he is to command the respect, not only of the diners, but also of his colleagues and superiors.

The personal attributes of a waiter may be classified under three headings, viz. physical, mental and moral qualities. Each of these attributes has an effect on his relationship with one or more of the three groups of people mentioned above (diners, colleagues and management).

2.1.1 PHYSICAL QUALITIES

In view of the necessity of working on one's feet for many hours at a time, usually on carpeted floors, and in enclosed situations which are often hot and stuffy, especially in the summer months, it is extremely important that waiting staff have stamina, and keep themselves as fit as possible, taking exercise and plenty of fresh air when off duty.

2.1.1.1 Personal attributes

Personal hygiene. The very nature of the job brings the body of the waiter into very close contact (within 30 cms or less) to the diners. Lack of personal hygiene will most certainly offend a diner who is about to enjoy a meal. Even colleagues will try to avoid working with anyone with poor personal hygiene, resulting in lack of harmony in the workplace, which may become a matter of concern for the management.

Appearance. The first impression of a waiter is gained by his appearance, and this impression lasts in the mind of the diner throughout his stay. Colleagues who take pride in their jobs (and their appearance) would be reluctant to work with others who do not come up to their standard, thus affecting team spirit.

Punctuality. Colleagues are most affected by lack of punctuality in others, because they will resent doing '*mise-en-place*' tasks for someone else.

If it were a frequent occurrence, management would view it seriously, and may wish to take disciplinary action, and, of course, diners will experience inefficiency in the service, and be subjected to delays.

Speech. Diners expect waiters to be polite, courteous and pleasant, and nothing less will do. A waiter, therefore, must make a conscious effort to develop a clear manner of speech because communication in his job is generally of a verbal nature.

Handwriting. A waiter should make every effort to develop good, legible handwriting because the orders that he takes will have to be read by the kitchen staff and the cashier. Illegible handwriting may result in delayed service, wrong orders being prepared or mistakes on the diners' bills. This will eventually make unnecessary additional work for colleagues, and cause annoyance to the customers.

2.1.2 MENTAL QUALITIES

Memory. People like to be recognised – it makes them feel important. A waiter should therefore cultivate a good memory for faces. An effort should also be made to remember the names of diners, at least those who visit the restaurant frequently. The other vital and important side of using memory is in remembering the orders of individual diners. Repeating back the order to diners not only clarifies and confirms, but also assists in remembering individual orders.

Knowledge of food and drink. A waiter must have adequate knowledge of the food and drink served in the establishment. Thus a waiter should be able to describe all menu items to the diner in simple terms.

2.1.3 MORAL QUALITIES

Honesty. Honesty is the basis of trust. Honesty to diners, colleagues and management is all-important to create a good, relaxed and efficient working environment.

Confidentiality. Many diners discuss matters of personal and confidential nature during meals which may be overheard by the waiter in the course of his duties. Such information should always be kept confidential. A waiter should make no deliberate effort to overhear the conversations of the diners, and on no account should he pass comment on what may have been said, or heard, unless expressly requested to do so by the diner, and comments that he might make should be calculated not to give offence. It is always best policy not to be drawn into this sort of situation.

Discretion.   A good waiter will never assume that a diner's partner is, or is not, his spouse. It is always the best approach to call a female guest 'Madam' rather than 'Mrs . . .'. This will avoid causing any embarrassment to any of the parties concerned.

2.1.4 'LANGUAGE' AND ADDRESSING PEOPLE'

A good waiter, as well as being skilful in the service of food should be capable of dealing with guests in a friendly and diplomatic manner without being servile or overfamiliar, yet at the same time carrying out his secondary, though no less important role as salesman and representative of the establishment.

It is always good policy to discover the names of regular clients and to greet them with their names when seating them, but after that the use of 'sir' or 'madam' is always acceptable.

Waiters should always exercise discretion, and never join in diners' conversation or pass any comment on what may have been said at the table, unless asked by the diner, and even in this case great care must be taken over the answer so as not to appear to 'take sides' over any contentious matter no matter how trivial it may appear to the waiter.

Proper use should be made of any diner's title etc, but after greeting them in the proper fashion then 'sir' or 'madam' is quite in order normally, but this would depend much on the individual diner, and the waiter must use his experience to judge what form of address would be acceptable to any particular individual.

A knowledge of at least one foreign language is always useful in waiting staff, with French probably being the most useful, since most restaurants still use many French terms on menus and, to a certain extent French is a 'tool of the trade'. Many customers will expect the waiter to be able to explain to them the content of dishes.

To this end, if for no other, a waiter should try to develop a pleasant mode of speech and clarity of expression. Knowledge of methods of cooking and menu terms is essential and use of such phrases as 'you know' when explaining to diners is meaningless, as, if they did know, they would have no need to ask in the first place! Care must be taken to use the form 'Would you like . . .?' rather than 'Do you want . . .?'

2.1.5   GUEST RELATIONSHIPS

The most important element which contributes to the enjoyment of good food is the treatment which the diner receives from the waiter.

Before looking at guest relationships, it is important to understand one basic fact. A waiter, irrespective of his colour or creed, is playing a 'role' and therefore his behaviour must conform to the understood image of that role.

The relationship of a waiter with a diner may be summarised in three words: Short; Formal; Professional.

This relationship should be kept on a purely formal basis, as cordial as possible, without being too familiar, even if the diner is awkward or rude. In these circumstances it is better to ignore such behaviour rather than make an issue of it.

Relationships with diners must always be kept on a professional basis, and waiters should never get themselves involved in the personal problems of diners.

2.2   SERVICE SKILLS – MENTAL

Apart from the memory element involved in the social skills area, eg remembering guests's names etc, there is a large area of mental skill involved in the recognition and identification of all the different items used in the day-to-day work of the waiter and the mental processes used in the serving and portioning of dishes and the calculation of bills.

2.2.1   *TABLES, CHAIRS AND RESTAURANT FURNITURE*

Tables

Tables in general use in restaurants are of three shapes, square, rectangular and round, and depending on the type and size employed, one must allow a minimum of $2\frac{1}{2}$ feet (750 mm) per diner.

In high-class restaurants, circular tables are preferred, because they can be used for 1, 2, 3, or 4 diners, according to size, and they can be placed symmetrically without looking 'regimented'.

Larger sizes of round tables may be used for larger numbers, as follows:

Persons	Minimum	Diameter
1	2 ft 6 in	750 mm
2–3	3 ft–3 ft 3 in	1000 mm
4	3 ft–3 ft 3 in	1000 mm
5–6	4 ft	1250 mm
2–9	5 ft	1500 mm
10	5 ft 9 in	1800 mm
12	8 ft	2000 mm

Square tables are usually 3 ft square (900 mm) or $2\frac{1}{2}$ ft square (750 mm) – the smaller size being only adequate for 2 diners for à la carte or 4 for table d'hôte service.

The $2\frac{1}{2}$ ft size is useful with various sizes of removable round tops, or extension pieces (*allonges*) to make longer tables or other conformations for functions or banqueting. Extension pieces are usually made in modules either $2\frac{1}{4}$ or $4\frac{1}{2}$ ft lengths to allow for 1 or 2 diners to sit at them.

Various methods of fixing can be employed, ranging from wooden battens to patented hooking systems.

'D'-shaped extensions are also available to permit the seating of two diners at the end of such tables.

Rectangular tables for 4 diners are usually used with banquette seating and are normally 4 × $2\frac{1}{2}$ ft in size.

All dining tables are made to a height of either $2\frac{1}{3}$ ft (720 mm) or $2\frac{1}{2}$ ft (760 mm), the lower height being used with fully-upholstered seating, to allow for its springiness.

A range of modern banqueting tabling is shown in Figure 2.1.

2.2.1.2   *Seating*

Seating for restaurant usage is of many types, depending on the decor of the room that it is to be used in, and the type of operation being considered.

FIG. 2.1 Restaurant and modular banqueting tabling (G N Burgess & Co Ltd)

Seating can either consist of chairs of various types, or uphol-stered banquettes, which are usually used in popular catering situ-ations with small rectangular tables, to produce 'compartments' as found in Pullman cars.

Several factors must be considered, as follows:

Comfort of the diners.   This will depend on the type of restaurant, and in a luxury restaurant, comfortable, armed dining chairs will be provided. In a more popular type restaurant, chairs will be harder and less comfortable in an attempt to prevent diners from lingering too long at table and preventing a second sitting. In a fast-food restaurant, chairs will be simple, bordering on the uncomfortable to prevent any sense of comfort, for the same reason as before.

Cover material used should be capable of being cleaned easily and woven material with an open weave is not considered suitable for restaurant use. A man-made fibre velvet, such as 'Dacron' which can be easily sponged clean, is ideal if a woven covering is wanted, otherwise a leather or simulated leather material can be used.

The angle between back and seat should be acute rather than obtuse to give support to the back.

Standard height for dining chair seats is 18 in. (450 mm). If upholstered, then the 'settled' height should be no more than 18 inches. This height gives a comfortable sitting position for eating and allows 9–10 in. (220–250 mm) space between top of chair and bottom of the table stile.

Ease of service. Restaurant chair-backs should be preferably narrower at the top than the bottom, rather than wider, to permit easy access between chairs for service purposes. The back should be high enough 2 ft 8 in. (800 mm) to give support to the back without impeding service.

Space taken up. Legs should preferably be perpendicular rather than splayed especially at the back to ease service, and an allowance of at least 2 ft 0 in. (610 mm) width for each diner should be made.

Chairs with arms should be so constructed that when not in use they do not stick out to their full depth of 16 in. (400 mm).

Chairs with the above features are shown in Figure 2.2.

FIG. 2.2 Modern 'Vars' metal-framed restaurant chair (G N Burgess & Co Ltd)

FIG. 2.3 Typical restaurant sideboards (2 styles) (Ward, Roper)

2.2.1.3   Sideboards

These are also known as 'dollies' or 'dumb-waiters'. A sideboard is a most important piece of restaurant furniture. It is the base from which waiting staff work in the 'room' and should therefore carry all the equipment necessary for use during the course of the meal.

The size and design will vary from one establishment to another, but its salient features should be the same, varying only due to type of menu or number of covers to be served from it.

It should have a flat unencumbered top to permit the unloading of the largest tray likely to be used in the establishment.

Below the top are drawers or 'pigeon-holes' to take service or other cutlery, under which in turn, are two or three shelves, to take other necessary equipment. Some sideboards will have a cupboard on one side in which soiled linen can be placed during the service.

In order to permit easy cleaning of floor surfaces and increase flexibility of the restaurant in use, it is a good feature to have castors on the sideboards. Typical sideboards as shown in Figure 2.3.

2.2.2   GENERAL-USE CUTLERY

Cutlery for general use can be made of base metal which is then silver plated, or completely made of stainless steel, from which all knife blades in general use are made. A typical pattern of cutlery is shown in Figure 2.4 (with a 1-ft rule for comparison) and indicates

FIG. 2.4 General use cutlery with relative sizes

from left to right: dessert knife; joint knife; fish knife; dessert fork; joint fork; fish fork; dessert spoon; soup spoon; coffee spoon; tea spoon.

2.2.2.1 *Service spoon and fork*

These are what are generally known as *table spoon* and *table fork* and are used for the service of various dishes. It is extremely important that the ends of the handles should match each other and be preferably flat to allow easy manipulation.

2.2.3 *GENERAL-USE CROCKERY*

Crockery in use in restaurants is usually based on earthenware, except in the most luxurious establishments, where bone china might be used.

Earthenware is made by baking potter's clay at a high temperature. Left in this state it is extremely porous and is therefore glazed, any decoration being put on under the glaze.

Porcelain, or bone china is made from a base of china clay to which is added ground bone, and it is then baked before being glazed. It is then glazed and baked again which produces a white porcelain with a transparent glaze, the whole being translucent. Decoration is added after the first glaze.

Food is served on several sizes and types of plates. Main courses are usually served on a plate of approximately 10 in. (250 mm). Entrées, sweets and fish (when served as a separate course), and sometimes hors-d'oeuvre, are served on a plate of approximately $8\frac{1}{2}$ in. (220 mm).

Most soups, as well as mussels, Irish stew and Lancashire hot-pot are served in a 9 in. (230 mm) soup plate with a 10 in. (250 mm) plate as an underliner.

A $6\frac{1}{2}$ in. or 7 in. (180 mm) plate is used for the service of cheese, bread rolls, afternoon tea and fruit.

A salad crescent or half-moon shaped plate is used for the service of side salads and is placed adjacent to the top left-hand corner of a joint plate 10 in. (250 mm).

Cereal bowls usually measure $7-7\frac{1}{2}$ in. (190 mm) and are used for porridge and cereals at breakfast, or for milk puddings, stewed fruits etc at other meals.

Oval platters measure approximately 12×10 in. (300×250 mm) and are used mainly for the service of grills such as steaks, chops etc, and whole fish such as sole or plaice.

A tea-cup contains approximately 7 fl oz (180 ml) and is used

FIG. 2.5(a) General use crockery styles (Steelite International plc)

with a matching saucer for the service of tea after meals, service of hot beverages (tea or coffee) at other times, eg mid-morning or afternoon.

A demi-tasse contains approximately 4 fl oz (100 ml) and is used with a matching saucer for the service of coffee after meals.

Soup cups or consommé cups usually have two handles and a matching saucer. Capacity is 10 fl oz (300 ml) and is used for the service of hot or cold soups or consommés.

All the above items are illustrated in Figure 2.5(a).

A modern shape is shown in Figure 2.5(b).

FIG. 2.5(b) Steelite 'Country Club' range (Steelite International plc)

Beer, Lager & Cider

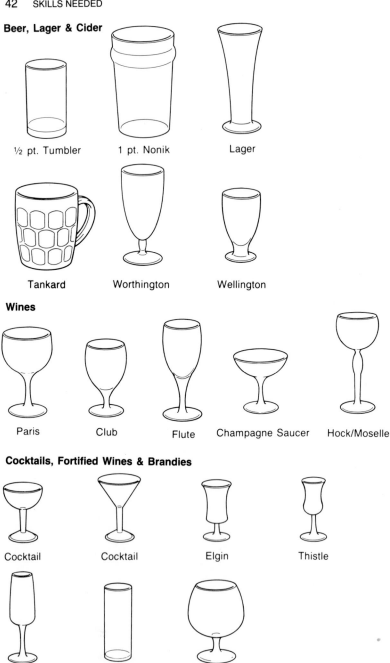

½ pt. Tumbler   1 pt. Nonik   Lager

Tankard   Worthington   Wellington

Wines

Paris   Club   Flute   Champagne Saucer   Hock/Moselle

Cocktails, Fortified Wines & Brandies

Cocktail   Cocktail   Elgin   Thistle

Copita   Slim Jim/Highball   Brandy Balloon

FIG. 2.6 General-use glassware

2.2.4 GENERAL-USE GLASSWARE

Glassware used in the restaurant may be classified under the following categories:

1. Beer, lager or cider glasses
2. Tankards
3. Glasses for still wines
4. Glasses for champagne and sparkling wines
5. Glasses for cocktails
6. Glasses for fortified wines and liqueurs
7. Glasses for spirits with mixers
8. Glasses for brandies and cognacs
9. Glasses for aperitifs, fruit juices and soft drinks*

* For these drinks a general purpose glass such as a Paris goblet is usually used.

It must be noted that patterns of different manufacturers vary, but the characteristics remain the same. Typical shapes are shown in Figure 2.6.

2.2.5 SPECIAL-USE CUTLERY

Under the heading of special-use cutlery will come the following:

1. Fruit knife and fork
2. Oyster fork
3. Lobster pick
4. Asparagus tongs
5. Snail fork
6. Grapefruit spoon
7. Ice cream spoon
8. Cheese knife
9. Sea-food fork
10. Cake fork/Pastry fork
11. Lobster crackers or krax
12. Caviare knife
13. Snail tongs
14. Corn-on-the-cob holders
15. Butter knife
16. Sundae spoon
17. Skewer for kebabs

These are illustrated in Figure 2.7(a), (b) & (c) and Figure 2.7(d) shows the relative sizes.

2.26 SPECIAL-USE CROCKERY

Under the above heading will come:

1. Sole dish
2. Gratin dish
3. Petite marmite
4. Scallop dish
5. Ramekin
6. Hors-d'oeuvre dish or ravier
7. Oeuf sur le plat dish
8. Consommé cup and saucer
9. Cocotte
10. Eggcups, double and single

Apart from items 8 and 10 which may match the normal-use crockery, all the others will be made of fireproof porcelain; as shown in Figure 2.8.

FIG. 2.7(a) Special-use cutlery: *Top*: pastry fork; oyster fork, Lobster pick; Asparagus tongs; *Bottom*: Snail tongs

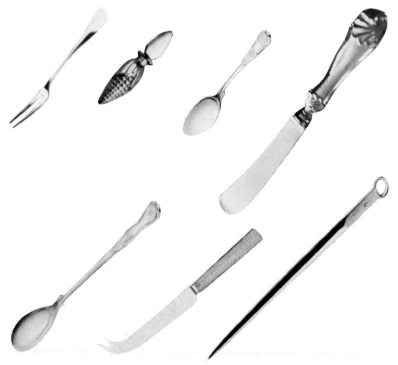

FIG. 2.7(b) Special-use cutlery: *Top*: Snail fork: Corn-on-the-cob holder; grapefruit spoon; butterknife   *Bottom*: sundae spoon; cheese knife; skewer

FIG. 2.7(c) Special-use cutlery: sea-food cocktail fork

Flatware Item Guide

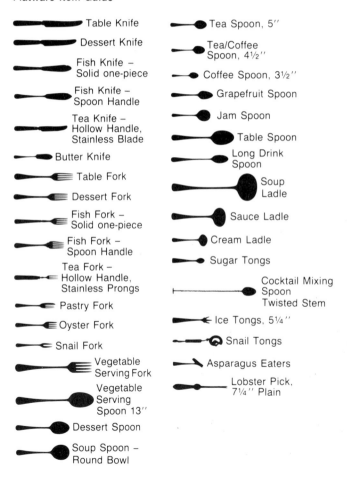

FIG. 2.7(d) Special-use cutlery: silhouette (Arthur Price of England)

FIG. 2.8 Special-use crockery

FIG. 2.9 Special-use glassware

2.2.7   SPECIAL-USE GLASSWARE

This category includes the following as shown in Figure 2.9.

1. Knickerbocker Glory glass
2. Coupes
3. Banana split dishes
4. Ashtrays
5. Oil and Vinegar cruets
6. Finger bowls

It must be noted that with the exception of items 1, 3 and 5 some establishments may use EPNS or stainless steel for these items.

2.2.8   SPECIAL-USE SERVICE EQUIPMENT

Under this heading are included the following items shown in Figure 2.10.

1. Grape scissors
2. Gateau slice or pastry server
3. Ice tongs
4. Sugar tongs
5. Poultry scissors
6. Nutcrackers
7. Lemon Press
8. Flambé or flare lamp
9. Flambé pan or chafing dish
10. Tea pot
11. Hot-water jug
12. Milk jug
13. Sugar bowl
14. Coffee pot
15. Cruet set
16. Sugar shaker or dredger
17. Pepper mill
18. Butter dish and drainer
19. Tea strainer
20. Duck press

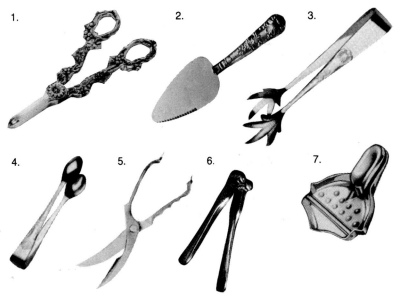

1. 2. 3. 4. 5. 6. 7.

FIG. 2.10

8.

9.

11.

10.

14.

12.

13.

FIG. 2.10 Contd

15.

16.

17.

18.

19.

FIG. 2.10 Contd   20.

2.2.9 SERVICE DISHES (KITCHEN)

The shape and size of service dishes will depend on the dish and number of portions being served.

Round flats.   Used for sliced meats with garnish, certain vegetables and sweets.

Oval flats.   Used for omelets, cutlets, fish fillets, and sliced, garnished meats.

Oval fish flats.   For whole grilled or poached round fish (trout, herring).

Entrée dishes.   Used for ragoûts, blanquettes etc., containing much sauce.

Soup tureens and individual soup servers.   For the service of soups. Cold soups (eg vichyssoise) may be served in a double timbale with a liner, crushed ice being placed between the two sections.

Vegetable dishes.   May be round or oval, plain or divided into two or more sections, depending on the quantity of vegetables ordered.

Note: All the above dishes are supplied from the kitchen with covers, except when used for deep fried items.

Sauce-boats.   These come in various sizes and are always presented on an underliner, although some have an integral underliner. Most sauces are served using a sauce ladle or spoon.

A range of typical items is shown in Figure 2.11.

2.2.10   SERVICE DISHES (SPECIAL)

Snail dish.   These can be obtained with either 6 or 12 indentations as determined by the portion size offered on the menu.

Oyster dish.   There are two types, one in which the oysters are placed on a bed of crushed ice with a half lemon placed in the centre, and the other type is similar, but has a liner with either 6 or 9 holes, in which the oysters are placed, crushed ice being placed beneath the liner.

Seafood cocktail cup and liner.   These are used for serving seafood cocktails, with crushed ice being placed between the outer and inner liner.

Coupes.   These are used for the service of ice-creams, grapefruit etc.

FIG. 2.11(a) General-use service equipment (kitchen): (l. to r.): Round flat; oval meat flat; oval fish flat; entrée dish: Round stackable cloche; oval stackable cloche; oval cloche; entrée dish

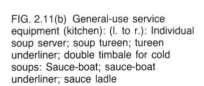

FIG. 2.11(b) General-use service
equipment (kitchen): (l. to r.): Individual
soup server; soup tureen; tureen
underliner; double timbale for cold
soups: Sauce-boat; sauce-boat
underliner; sauce ladle

FIG. 2.11(c) General-use service equipment (kitchen): (l. to r.): Single oval veg. dish; cover; Single round veg. dish; cover: Double oval veg. dish; double round veg. dish; triple veg. dish; quadruple veg. dish

FIG. 2.12 Special-use service dishes:
(l. to r.): Snail dish (12-hole); oyster
dish; oyster dish with separators;
seafood cocktail cup: Coupe;
avocado dish; toast racks

Avocado dish.   Used for the service of avocado pear halves.

Toast racks.   Toast racks are used for the service of breakfast toast in order to prevent the condensation causing the toast to lose its crispness.

A range of typical items is shown in Figure 2.12.

2.2.11   RESTAURANT LINEN

In these days, the use of the word 'linen' is often a misnomer, since most restaurant table and other linen is usually made either from cotton or a mixture of cotton and polyester, due mainly to initial high cost, cost of replacement, ease of washing, and so on. As many establishments now operate their own on-premises laundry (OPL), the ease of handling is very important.

Basic sizes of linen required will depend on the sizes of tables used, bearing in mind the need for a drop of at least 1 ft, (305 mm) on each side, thus a table 3 × 3 ft (914 × 914 mm) will require a cloth of 5 × 5 ft (1800 × 1800 mm), and for a 3-ft round table, a square cloth of sides 5 ft 6 in. (1900 mm).

For rectangular tables, or for use in banqueting situations, where tables are usually 2 ft 6 in. (760 mm) wide, cloths of 4 ft 6 in. (1375 mm) width and of various lengths are normally kept.

Serviettes are usually some 20 in. (510 mm) for dinner use, with smaller ones being used at breakfast.

Slip cloths (to cover light soiling between services etc), are normally 3 ft (914 mm) square.

Table linen is, by tradition, white, but colours are used in some establishments to tone with décor, or for special occasions (eg gold for golden weddings).

Waiter's cloths are usually 30 × 18 in. (760 × 460 mm) and made of cotton huckaback, or re-made from worn table cloths. Glass cloths should always be made from pure linen in order not to leave lint on clean glasses.

Cloths for other purposes, such as covering sideboards, etc, are often remade from old table cloths by the linen room.

2.2.12   WAITERS' CHECKS, BILLS, BAR CHECKS

The types of checks and bills used in an establishment will depend on the type of system adopted, based on the menu to be offered. Several of the most common types are ilustrated in Figure 2.13. and their method of use will be found in section 4.4.

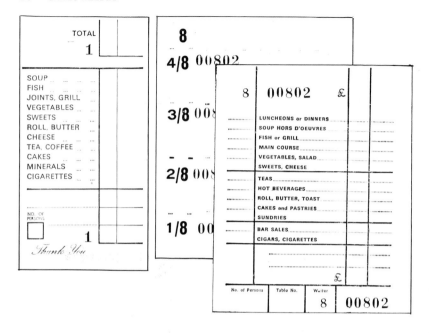

FIG. 2.13(a) Waiters' checks, bills and bar checks: *Top* (l. to r.): Cafe or tea-room check; Restaurant check with separate kitchen checks (perforated and numbered) *Bottom*: Waiter's summary sheet (for daily business done)

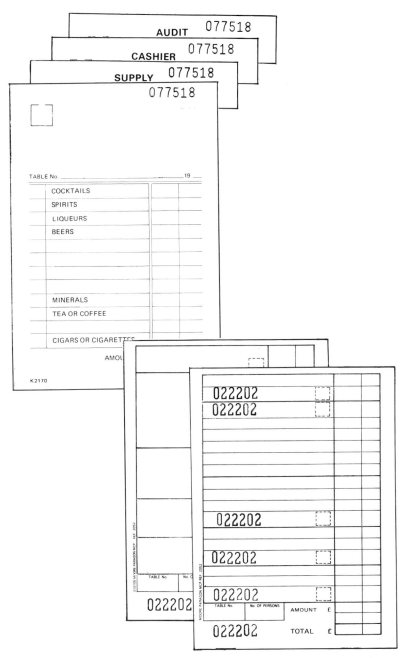

FIG. 2.13(b) Waiters' checks, bill and bar checks (l. to r.): Quadruplicated bill/check for use with Paragon multi-part machines; Bill with perforated kitchen checks (self-carbonised)

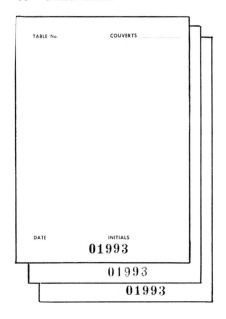

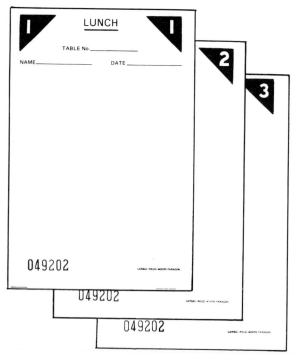

FIG. 2.13(c) Waiters' checks, bills and bar checks: Triplicate checking system checks (22 types)

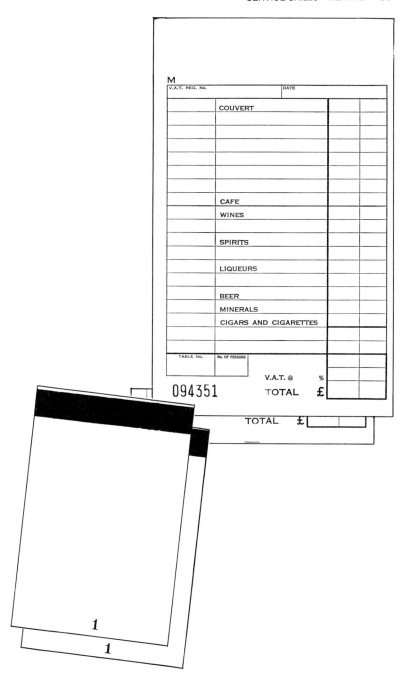

FIG. 2.13(d) Waiters' checks, bills and bar checks (l. to r.): Duplicate check for bar use; Duplicate bill for use with triplicate checking system

ORDER No. **14**

	Regular	Large	Supersize
1 TOMATO & CHEESE			
2 ONION			
3 MUSHROOM			
4 PEPPER			
5 VEGETARIAN			
6 ONION & PEPPER			
7 ONION & BLACK OLIVE			
8 HAM			
9 PEPPERONI SAUSAGE			
10 HAM & MUSHROOM			
11 ANCHOVY			
12 MUSHROOM & ANCHOVY			
13 PRAWN			
14 SPECIAL			
15 HOT ONE			
16 HAWAIIAN			
17 SOFT DRINKS			
18			
19			

TOTAL

TAKEN BY_____   No. OF PIZZA'S _____

ENJOY YOUR
PIZZA

MOORE PARAGON UK LTD

ORDER No.
14

HAVE A NICE
DAY PLEASE
CALL AGAIN

No:

RESTAURANT – Dissection Sheet

Day: Meal: Lunch/Dinner Weather: First Bill No:
                                    Float Total:£

Date: / /8 . Cashier:

BILL NO	TABLE No	CVRS	FOOD		DRINKS		COFFEE		TOTAL	
			MEALS	EXTRAS						
			£ p	£ p	£ p		£ p		£ p	
TOTALS										

ALL BILLS ARE TO BE INCLUDED EVEN IF VOID OR CANCELLED

CASH BILLS UNPAID	DIFFERENCE +/-	CASH TAKINGS	Less SUB-TOTAL	Less FLOAT	SUB-TOTAL £	1p	2p	5p	10p	20p	50p	COINS	£1	£1	£5	£10	£20	£50	NOTES	CHEQUES TOTAL £	GRAND TOTAL A+B	SUB-TOTAL £	COFFEE £	DRINKS £	EXTRAS £	FOOD £	ITEM
																						A					CASH
																				CASH SUMMARY		B					HOSPITALITY

FIG. 2.13(e) Waiters' checks, bills and bar checks: Typical cashier's dissection sheet/summary sheet for use with triplicate or other written checking systems

FIG. 2.13(f) Waiters' checks, bills and bar checks: Bill/check for use in pizza restaurant or other with restricted menu (opposite)

2.2.13   *RESTAURANT HEAVY EQUIPMENT*

Under this heading the names of most of the items being self-explanatory require no further explanation, but where description is necessary it is given:

1. Hors-d'oeuvre trolley
2. Pastry or sweet trolley
3. Carving trolley
4. Liqueur trolley
5. Réchaud or battery plate-warmer (This replaces the older type electric or spirit-lamp heated flat plate type of réchaud.)
6. Guéridon (lit. a small wheeled side-table) This has now become a trolley with a built-in lamp for preparing flambé dishes.
7. Wine cooler and stand
8. Cake stand
9. Serving trolley
10. Cheese trolley

All items are illustrated in Figure 2.14.

2.2.14   *USING BASIC MENTAL SKILLS*

A waiter must try to develop mental skills for two main purposes in his work, as follows:

Memory – (see also section 2.1.2).

Arithmetic – in order to be able to calculate diners' bills correctly, and also for portioning dishes; eg, a knowledge of methods of dividing a gâteau into a given number of equal portions (if this has not been done by the kitchen) requires a knowledge of angles, or being able to divide by two for even numbers of portions.

A relevant book that can be recommended for improvement of mental arithmetic skills is *Calculations for the Hotel and Catering Industry*, GE Gee (Arnold), 1980.

2.3   SERVICE SKILLS – PHYSICAL

2.3.1   *POSTURE AT SIDEBOARD*

The fundamental part of a waiter's job is 'to wait', ie to wait to anticipate and fulfil the needs of a diner. A waiter, when not actually engaged in service tasks should stand by his own sideboard, because that is the first place that a diner is likely to look for a waiter should he need service.

FIG. 2.14(a) Restaurant heavy equipment: *Top* (3): Carving trolley; (5) Réchaud or battery plate-warmer;   *Bottom* (l. to r.): (7) Wine cooler and stand; (8) Cake stand

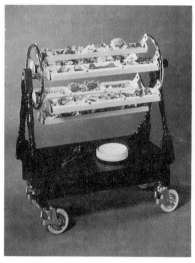

FIG. 2.14(b) (left) Hors-d'oeuvre trolley (Ward, Roper)

FIG. 2.14(c) (right) Sweet trolley (Ward, Roper)

FIG. 2.14(d) (left) Liqueur trolley (Ward, Roper)

FIG. 2.14(e) (right) Flambé trolley (Ward, Roper)

FIG. 2.14(f) (left) Guéridon or mobile dumb-waiter (Ward, Roper)

FIG. 2.14(g) (right) Cheese trolley (Ward, Roper)

During the service of a meal there can be long periods when a waiter must stand at his sideboard. Incorrect posture can not only be unsightly, but more important it can be very tiring, resulting in unnecessary fatigue. The routine for this is listed below, and the stance is illustrated in Figure 2.15.

1. Select a suitable spot by the sideboard so as not to obstruct other service staff, and yet be conspicuous to most customers.
2. *Stand straight and 'tall', with feet apart (about 6 inches), distributing the body weight evenly on both legs.*
3. † *Neatly fold and hang waiter's cloth near the wrist of the left forearm, bent at the elbow and at waist level.*
4. Right arm hanging straight down.
5. Look alert. This is easily achieved by observing the progress of the meals of the diners at the table(s) and looking for and anticipating their needs.

* *Standing with body weight on one leg may seem easier, but in actual fact it causes more fatigue, especially in the back.*
† *Refer to 'Using a waiter's cloth effectively (pp 98–102).*

FIG. 2.15 Posture at the sideboard

2.3.2 'CARRYING PLATES'

Stack of plates

Before the commencement of the service it may be necessary to carry stacks of plates to prepare sideboards. A waiter should be able to carry 10–12 plates with ease.

Method
1. Check that the plates are of the same size and shape and that the stack is stable.
2. Prepare the stack on a safe surface at about waist height.
3. Insert the fingers, slightly spread apart, under either side of the stack and support the side of the stack with the palms of the hands, as shown in Figure 2.16.
4. Gently but firmly lift the stack and hold it against the body at waist height, or slightly lower if comfortable.
5. Carry stack to the required place, opening doors with the back or foot, using kick-plate or bar.
6. Place the stack on the required shelf by bending from the knees (not the waist!), or lifting up the stack by bending the elbows.

Note: It is not safe working practice to attempt to place stacks of plates on surface higher than chest-level!

FIG. 2.16 Carrying stack of plates

FIG. 2.17 Carrying plates during the service

During the service of the meal, it will be necessary to carry hot plates from the sideboard to the table, using the routine below and referring to Figure 2.17.

1. Place folded waiter's cloth over the plates.
2. Using the left hand, slide one end of the waiter's cloth under the stack keeping the hand under the cloth.
3. Using the right hand and the other end of the waiter's cloth, slide the stack onto the left fore-arm and hand, keeping the waiter's cloth between the stack and the forearm.

Carrying three plates with food

In the 'popular' type of restaurants, the service of food may be plated. In such cases the waiter requires the skills of carrying maximum number of plates to cut down the number of 'trips' between service point and the tables.

Method

1. Pick up the first plate in the right hard, thumb on the rim, and fingers underneath. Keep the plate level.
2. Transfer plate to the left hand on fingers 1 and 2, thumb on the rim and fingers 3 and 4 crooked upwards, (as for clearing plates), as in Figure 2.18.

FIG. 2.18 Carrying one plate with food

3. Pick up the second plate and place on the heel of the thumb and the tips of fingers 3 and 4 of the left hand. Ensure that both plates are safely balanced and kept level, as in Figure 2.19.

FIG. 2.19 Carrying two plates with food

FIG. 2.20 Carrying three plates with food

4. Pick up the third plate in the right hand, (as in step 1), as shown in Figure 2.20.
5.*Approach the table to the right of the diner to be served right foot forward.
6. Keep the plates on the left hand away from the body, behind the diner's back.
7. Make the diner aware that you are about to place the plate in front of him. (Most diners will bend to their left to allow easy access)
8.† Place the plate by gently lowering it onto the table.
9. Step back and move to the right of the next diner.
10. Take the second plate from the left to the right hand, and repeat steps 7 and 8.
11. Repeat steps 9 and 10 for the third diner.

2.3.3 USING A TRAY

Trays are basic tools of the food service staff for transporting items

---

* When walking with three plates it may be necessary to give a slight sideways swing to the plates in the left hand, to compensate for the walking motion.
† In case of plated main course make sure that the plate is placed in such a way that the meat is nearest to the diner.

of crockery, silver, food etc. Correct and efficient use of trays reduces 'fatigue' by cutting down the number of 'trips' between the place of collection and the destination.

Trays come in different sizes to suit different loads. They are usually rectangular or round in shape and can be made from metal or resin-filled wood. Small round trays are usually used for the service of drinks or small items at the table. Small and medium trays may be carried on the forearm and hand, but large trays will need to be carried with both hands.

Always select a tray of suitable size for the load to be carried. Too large a tray will allow unnecessary movement of items whereas too small a tray may cause unsafe stacking of items thus making it accident prone.

The skill in using a tray is mainly that of balancing the tray and maintaining the balance while carrying. Thus a tray must be loaded sensibly and logically so that it is easy to balance.

Unless the tray has a non-slip surface to prevent certain items from slipping on the tray surface it may be necessary to line the tray with a tray coth or paper serviette.

Small and medium trays
It is easier and safer to balance these trays on a forearm and hand by placing the length of the tray on the arm.

Method
1. Place the tray on a suitable and safe surface not higher than your waist.
2. Load the tray, placing heavier items nearest to yourself (as shown in Figure 2.21.)
3. Put left foot forward and position the left forearm and hand level with the tray. Bend from the waist and knee, if necessary.
4. Firmly but gently pull the tray with the right hand drawing it onto the left hand and forearm so that the nearest edge of the tray is at the end of the forearm and the far end still rests on the surface.
5. Take the load on the forearm, balance on spread fingers and palm, adjust position of the tray with the right hand to ensure proper balance, as in Figure 2.22.
6. Straighten up and carry at waist level. (Do not rest elbow on waist or stomach)
7. On reaching the destination place the tray on a suitable surface by positioning the tray level with the surface, gently resting the far edge of the tray on the surface and pushing the tray to slide

FIG. 2.21 Loading tray

FIG. 2.22 Carrying tray

onto the surface. (Do not attempt to unload the tray without first placing it on a safe surface and checking that it will not overbalance.)

Large trays
The procedure for using large trays is as follows:
1. Load the tray by spreading the load evenly on the tray.

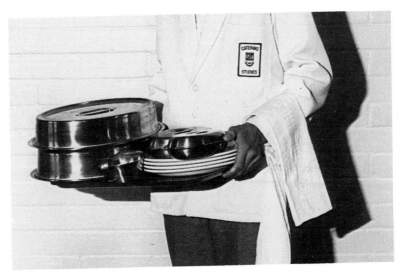

FIG. 2.23 Carrying large tray

2. Place one foot forward, bend at the waist and knee if necessary.
3. Hold edges of the tray firmly at about the centre of each side, as shown in Figure 2.23.
4. Lift tray. Ensure that the load is not excessive for the journey length.
5. Straighten up, holding the tray at waist level well away from the body. Do not rest elbows on waist or stomach.

2.3.4 CARRYING GLASSES

For stemmed glasses it is quicker and easier to carry them hanging between the fingers, as described below, but this task must be performed carefully as any carelessness may result in broken glass causing unnecessary work. In the presence of diners, however, *all* glasses *must* be carried on a service salver.

Method
1. Starting with the glasses upside down (bowl downwards), pick up the first glass by holding the base between the first two fingers underneath and thumb on top.
2. Transfer it to the left hand (palm uppermost) by placing the stem between fingers 1 and 2, allowing glass to hang, as in Figure 2.24.
3. Pick up the second glass as before, transferring it to the left hand

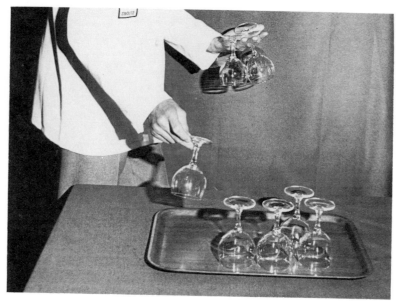

FIG. 2.24 Carrying glasses

FIG. 2.25 Carrying glasses

FIG. 2.26 Carrying glasses

between fingers 2 and 3. Slide the base of the second glass under the base of the first.

4. Similarly place the third glass between fingers 3 and 4, as in Figure 2.25.
5. Repeat the action placing each successive glass under the base of the preceding glass, utilising all fingers to full length, up to a maximum of 8 glasses.
6. Curl in the fingers slightly to prevent the glasses from knocking one another during movement; as shown in Figure 2.26.
7. Remove the glasses in the reverse order.

2.3.5   SERVING – USING ONE SPOON

Certain food items such as accompaniments are served using one spoon only. Although the fundamental skill of using a spoon is the same, the service of these food items may be divided into three types, each of which may need slightly different treatment, as follows:

(a) Powdery or granular, eg parmesan cheese, sugar, croûtons etc.
(b) Liquids, eg gravies or thin sauces
(c) Emulsified sauces, eg mayonnaise, tartare, hollandaise, etc.

The method of serving with one spoon only is described below and illustrated in Figure 2.27.

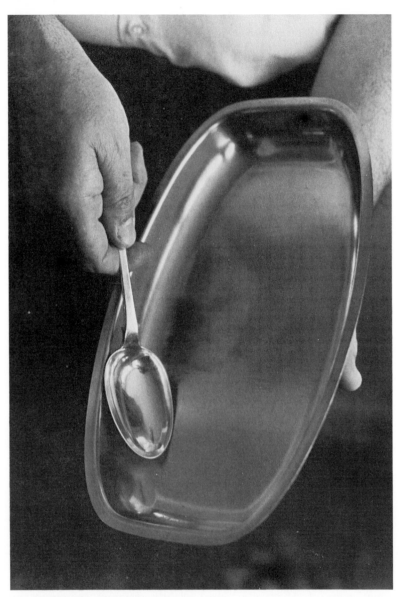

FIG. 2.27 Serving using one spoon

1. Hold the spoon with its handle in the palm and the centre of the handle between forefinger and thumb
2. Insert the spoon into the dish/sauce-boat, tip first.
3. Lift out the spoon collecting a quantity of the food in it, keeping it above the dish/sauce-boat to catch any surplus.

4. (a) Gently and discreetly shake the spoon to remove any surplus into the sauce-boat. (Do not hit the dish with the spoon.)

   (b) In case of liquids, if the spoon is full to the brim, return a little by tilting the spoon.

   (c) For emulsified sauces, gently wipe the underside of the spoon on the rim of the sauce-boat.

5. Serve onto the diner's plate by moving the spoon, keeping it level to within 1 cm above the food. Tilt the spoon slightly by turning the wrist anti-clockwise.

Powdery and granular items may be sprinkled with a gentle shake, gravies and thin sauces spooned over or 'napped', and emulsified sauces may require the spoon to be tilted more and given a gentle vertical shake.

2.3.6 SERVING – USING SPOON AND FORK

The combination of spoon and fork provides the most versatile tool for the service of food. Most dishes can be served with spoon and fork and food service staff take pride in their skill of manipulating spoon and fork for the service of a variety of dishes.

Service spoons and forks should be stored in the sideboard in pairs, keeping the curve of fork prongs in the bowls of the spoons.

Method

1. Pick up the spoon and fork together from near the middle of the handle using the tip of the first finger and the thumb as in Figure 2.28. Grip the base of the spoon and fork with fingers 3 and 4 while maintaining the balance by supporting the spoon with the second finger.

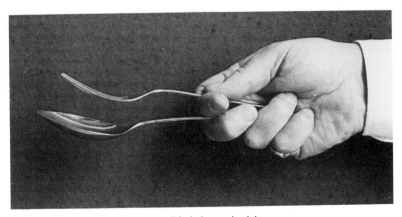

FIG. 2.28 Serving using spoon and fork (normal grip)

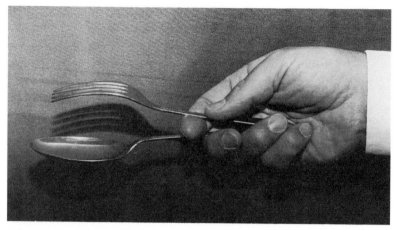

FIG. 2.29 Serving using spoon and fork (grip for round items)

2. Insert the tip of the first finger between the spoon and the fork handles and hold the fork handle between the tip of first finger and thumb.
3. (a)*Maintaining the grip on the base of the handles and keeping the balance of the spoon, lift the prongs of the fork up. Lower back into the bowl of the spoon.
   (b)†Slacken the grip at the base, and using the first finger and thumb turn the fork over, as in Figure 2.29.
   (c)‡Hold spoon and fork as in 2. Using the tip of the first finger and thumb, move the fork to the right of the spoon, as in Figure 2.30.

2.3.7 SERVING – USING TWO FISH KNIVES

Certain items, in particular poached and shallow-fried fish are best served using two fish knives. Other than holding the two knives correctly, the main skill is judging the 'gap' to be left between the two knives in relation to the size of the item to be served.

---

* The action is similar to that of using a pair of tongs. Flat pieces of food such as slices of meat etc. can be served with spoon and fork in this position.
† This position is most suited to round items such as rolls, potatoes, etc.
‡ This position is suitable for large flat items, such as fillets of fish or Spanish omelets, etc.

FIG. 2.30 Serving using spoon and fork (grip for large, flat items)

Method
1. Hold the two knives slightly spread apart, as shown in Figure 2.31.
2. Adjust the gap between the two knives so that it is approximately $\frac{1}{3}$ of the size of the item to be picked up.
3. Place the tips of the knives, slightly angled downward near the middle of the edge of the item to be picked up.
4. Gently but firmly push the knives under the item and at the same time bringing down the handles to make them horizontal.

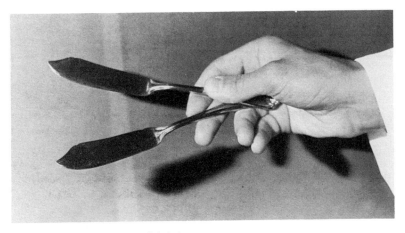

FIG. 2.31 Serving using two fish knives

5. Lift the item slightly, at the same time checking that it shows no sign of 'breaking-up', and that it is balanced on the knife blades. Adjust the position of the knives, if necessary.
6. Transfer the item to the diner's plate, keeping the knives level, lowering the item gently, at the same time raising the handles to create a 'slide' and withdraw the knives. (It may sometimes be necessary to give the knives a gentle, discreet shake to free the knives from the food and to withdraw.)

2.3.8   SERVING – USING ONE FORK

This procedure is used for long, thin slices of certain foods, especially thinly cut sliced cold meats, or smoked salmon.

The main advantage of this method is that better presentation of slices on the plate is achieved. The positioning of the fork is shown in Figure 2.32.

Method

1. Hold the centre of the handle with the thumb and forefinger, with the end of the handle resting loosely in the palm.
2. Turn the fork so that the prongs are vertical.
3. Insert the lowermost prong under the slice of food to be served, at the end nearest to yourself.
4. Twist the fork between the thumb and the forefinger, maintaining the balance, and rolling the slice of food onto the prongs of the fork.

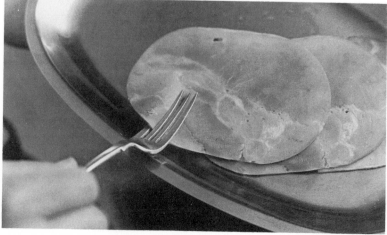

FIG. 2.32 Serving using one fork (stage 3)

FIG. 2.33 Serving using one fork (stage 4)

5. Lift the fork transferring it over the diner's plate, then unroll starting from the far side, as shown in Figure 2.33.

2.3.9 SERVING – USING TWO FORKS

The skill in using two forks for service is exactly the same as that for using two fish knives (see section 2.3.7). Because the service forks provide a much greater span, larger items such as a rolled omelet, or larger slices of meat should therefore be served using this technique, which is shown in Figure 2.34.

FIG. 2.34 Serving using two forks

2.3.10   SERVING – USING LADLE FROM A TUREEN

When more than one portion of soup is to be served at a table, the soup is supplied from the kitchen in a suitable-sized tureen. The waiter should collect the soup in the tureen from the kitchen, together with a ladle, hot soup-plates and 'liners', on a suitable, tray.

Method

1. Place soup tureen and plates on the sideboard, keeping the plates on the left-hand side of the tureen, close to the base. Remove the lid and place it upside-down to the right of the tureen.
2. Pick up ladle, holding it between first and second fingers and thumb of the right hand.
3. Dip the bowl of the ladle into the soup and stir gently to distribute the garnish (if any) in the soup.
4. Raise the full ladle clear of the soup, keeping the bowl of the ladle level, as shown in Figure 2.35.
5. Touch the base of the ladle onto the surface of the soup to remove any drips. (Alternatively, wipe the base of the ladle on the edge of the tureen to collect any drips.)
6. Raise the ladle just above the edge of the tureen and move the

FIG. 2.35 Serving using a ladle (tureen)

FIG. 2.36 Serving using a ladle (tureen)

ladle to the left, keeping the bowl of the ladle level, and position it over the centre of the soup-plate at a height of about 5 cm.
7. Tilt the ladle to allow the soup to run into the soup-plate, as in Figure 2.36.
8. Return the ladle to the tureen and repeat steps 3 to 7 until all the soup has been portioned into the plates.

Note: Refer also to 'Service of Soup' under 'Tasks during Service', see section 3.2.2.5. (p. 163–4).

2.3.11   SERVING – USING LADLE FROM A SAUCE-BOAT

Sauces and gravies in a sauce-boat should be served using a ladle. They should not be poured from the sauce-boat itself.

Method
1. Pick up the sauce-boat by its handle and place it on an underliner.
2. Place a ladle of suitable size on the underliner to the right hand side of the lip of the sauce-boat so that the handle of the ladle is opposite to the handle of the sauce-boat.
3. Place the underliner, sauce-boat and ladle onto a folded waiter's cloth on the palm of the left hand so that the handle of the ladle is facing forward.
4. Approach from the left of the customer, left foot forward.

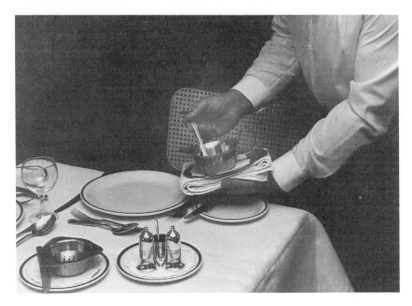

FIG. 2.37 Serving using a ladle (sauce-boat) (stage 3)

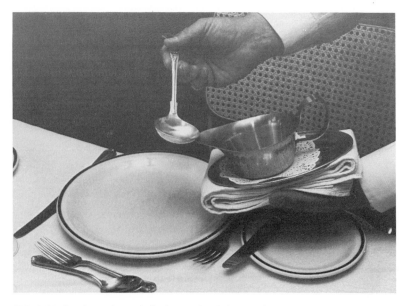

FIG. 2.38 Serving using a ladle (sauce-boat) (stage 4)

5. Pick up the ladle between first two fingers and thumb, with thumb on top of the handle, as in Figure 2.37.

6. Bend from the waist and move the left hand towards the customer's plate so that the underliner and sauceboat are above the customer's plate, but not obscuring your view.

7. Dip ladle into the sauce, lift clear and scrape the bottom of the ladle on the edge of the sauceboat, to avoid drips, as in Figure 2.38.

8. Move ladle towards plate, over the lip of the sauceboat, tilting the ladle to allow the sauce to run off.

9. Repeat steps 7 and 8 if more sauce is required.

10. Return ladle into the sauce, not onto the underliner.

11. Serve all diners, each time returning the ladle to the sauce-boat.

2.3.12 *SERVING FROM A SERVICE FLAT, DISH, OR PLATE*

Certain items of food such as slices of meat, prepared small cuts of meat, and fish are arranged appetisingly and decorated with appropriate garnishes on a suitable sized flat. The waiter must demonstrate the skill of presenting the food to the diners and serve it onto the diners' plates with the minimum disturbance to the attractive presentation of the food, and at the same time ensuring that all diners are served the correct portion. (The food is generally arranged on the flat so as to make obvious the size of each portion and the items of garnish to be served. If this is not the case, the waiter should check with the chef before bringing out the food into the restaurant.)

Method

1. With the left hand and forearm lined with the service cloth in the 'pad' form, carry the flat to the table. If the portions overlap, the top portion should be at the front of the flat, ie away from self.

2.*Pick up serving spoon and fork in the right hand, ready for service.

3. Approach the table to the left of the customer, with left foot forward.

4. Keeping the flat level, bend from the waist and present the food. Pause and let the diners have a view of the presentation. (The duration of the pause will depend on the interest created by the dish. The waiter must use his own judgment.)

---

* Refer to 'Serving using a spoon and fork', section 2.3.6.

FIG. 2.39 Serving from a dish, flat or plate

5. Hold the flat near the diner's plate about 10–15 cm above the table. Let the rim of the flat slightly overlap on the rim of the plate, as shown in Figure 2.39.
6. Slide the service spoon under the top portion (furthest from self), and using the spoon and fork, pick up the portion and briefly pause over the flat for any drips.
7. Using spoon and fork, serve any garnish.
8. Tilt the flat slightly forward so that the sauce or gravy collects at the front. Open spoon and fork by moving the fork to the right and spoon over sauce or gravy onto the portion.
9. Straighten up, take one step backwards and move to the left of the next diner. Repeat from step 4, each time serving the top portion, ie working from the front of the flat to back.

2.3.13 SERVING FROM A DEEP DISH

Dishes such as stews, ragoûts and blanquettes are supplied from the kitchen in deep dishes. The items of food are covered with gravy or sauce, and therefore the size of a portion is not obvious. In some cases the chef will be able to guide the waiter, in others the waiter must use his own judgment and experience in serving the portions.

The serving dish is normally supplied on an underliner. Where an underliner is not provided by the kitchen, the waiter should use a service plate.

FIG. 2.40 Serving from a deep dish

Method

1. Carry the dish on the left hand, on the service cloth folded in the 'pad' form.
2. Pick up the service spoon and fork in the right hand, ready for service.
3. Approach the table to the left of the diner, left foot forward.
4. Bend from the waist and hold the dish near to the diner's plate about 10–15 cm above the table.
5. Open the spoon and fork, slide spoon (using tip of spoon) under the portion and pick up the portion gripping it between spoon and fork, as in Figure 2.40.
6. Pause over the dish for drips, and serve onto the plate.
7. Repeat steps 5 and 6 until the correct-size portion has been served.
8. With the fork held open, spoon the sauce or gravy over the portion on the plate.
9. Straighten up and take one step backwards. Move to the left of the next diner and repeat from step 4 until all diners have been served.

Note: The important thing to learn is to apportion the food equally so that the last diner receives the right-size portion and a minimal quantity is left in the dish.

2.3.14   SERVING FROM A SALVER

Although, generally, a salver is used for transporting items of cutlery etc in the presence of the diners, it may be used for the service and clearing of dishes served in coupes, coffee, etc.

Service

1. Load the salver with a stack of sideplates with doilies, coupes, and teaspoons.
2. Approach the table, to the left of the diner to be served, carrying the loaded salver on a folded waiter's cloth on the left hand and forearm.
3. Using fingers 1 and 2 of the right hand, lift a coupe and place it on the top plate of the stack.
4. Place a spoon on the plate to the right of the coupe, as in Figure 2.41.
5. Place the prepared plate in front of the diner so that the spoon is on the right hand side of the diner.
6. Repeat steps 2 to 5 for each diner.

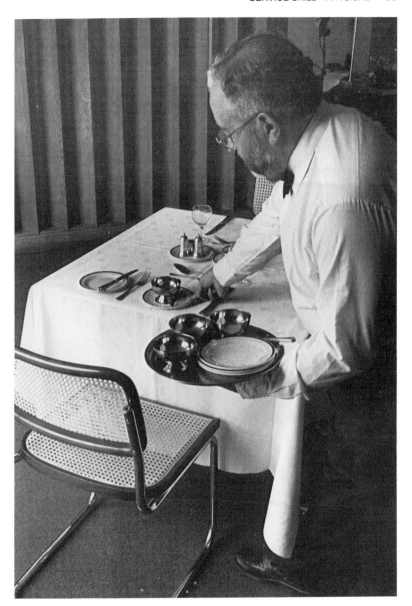

FIG. 2.41 Serving from a salver

Clearing
1. Pick up the salver on the left hand and forearm on a folded waiter's cloth.
2. Approach the table, from the right-hand side of the diner, right

foot forward, salver kept away from the body, behind the diner's back.

3. Pick up the sideplate with the coupe and spoon still on it.
4. Step back and place the set on the salver, on the part nearest to the body.
5. Remove spoon and place it to the right side of the plate, and the coupe to the other side, as in Figure 2.42.

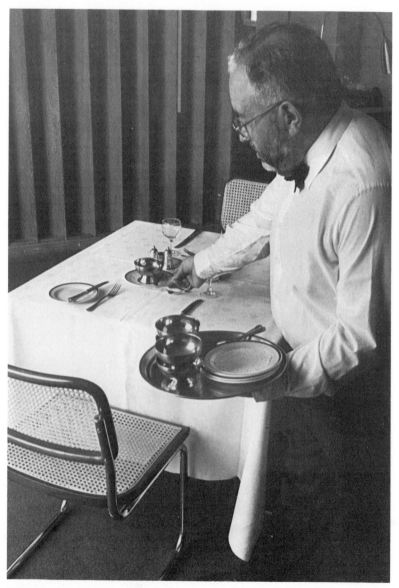

FIG. 2.42 Clearing with a salver

6. Move to the right of the next diner and pick up the sideplate with the coupe placing it on the sideplate already on the salver.
7. Repeat step 5.
8. Continue to repeat steps 2 to 5 for each diner until all have been cleared, stacking plates and spoons neatly. If necessary, stack coupes in twos.

Note:

1. It is important to maintain the balance of the salver at all times, if necessary adjusting the balance each time, before moving to the next diner.
2. The same procedures may be used for the service of coffee, replacing coupes by coffee cups.

2.3.15 SERVING FROM A TROLLEY, BUFFET, OR GUÉRIDON

Certain dishes such as hors-d'oeuvre, sweets or guéridon specialities are best served from the trolley or guéridon, which are normally designed to have space for loading and carrying a stack of plates on which to serve the food. This permits the waiter to use both hands for service.

The same principle applies to those restaurants which may have a buffet or cold display from which waiters will serve diners.

Method

1. Manoeuvre the trolley to the table and position it close to the table so that the diners may have a full and clear view of the food displayed on the trolley.
2. Allow the diners to make their choice.
3. Place a clean plate on the trolley or plate stand, and serve the diner's choice onto the plate using spoon and fork or special service equipment, arranging the items tastefully.
4. Pick up the plate in the right hand (fingers underneath, thumb on the rim.)
5. *Approach the diner from the right, right foot forward, and gently place the plate in front of the diner.
6. Repeat steps 3 to 5 for each diner. (Sometimes it may be necessary to move the trolley to the other side of the table to allow a better view of the food to enable them to make their choice.)

---

* Some establishments prefer food to be served from the left. In that case, approach the diner from the left, left foot forward.

2.3.16 *POLISHING CUTLERY*

Cutlery washed and drained in the wash-up area needs a final rubbing-up with a cloth to bring out its shine and remove any water-marks. Items of cutlery which are tarnished or have stubborn stains may need special cleaning (refer to section 1.4.2 pp 13–14).

Method
1. Collect washed and drained cutlery, a clean service tray, and sufficient service cloths for the task in hand. Sort the cutlery.
2. Open out service cloth and cover left hand with one corner of the cloth, half-closing the left hand to secure the cloth.
3. Pick up 8–10 pieces of cutlery with the right hand and place the handles of the cutlery in left hand on the cloth, as in Figures 2.43 and 2.44.*
4. Take the opposite corner of the service cloth in the right hand. Hold the bowl of the spoon in the cloth between thumb and fingers 1 and 2.
5. Hold the handle of the spoon with the thumb and first finger of left hand.

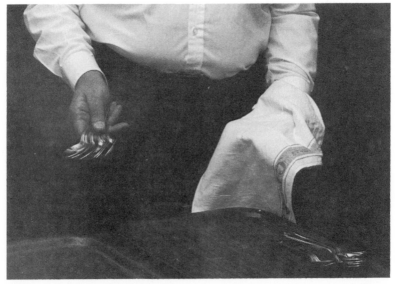

FIG. 2.43 Polishing cutlery (stage 1)

* Prongs of forks, or blades of knives, sharp edge facing away from self.

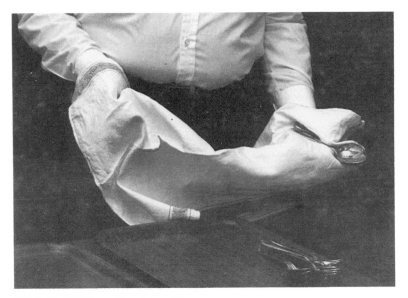

FIG. 2.44 Polishing cutlery (stage 2)

6. Polish the bowl and handle by rubbing with the cloth in the right hand, as in Figure 2.45.
7. Check that both sides are polished.

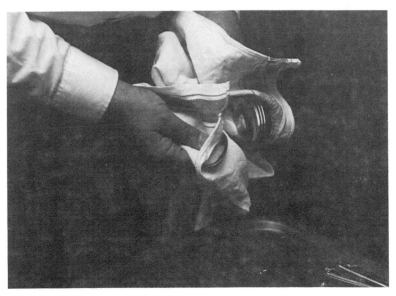

FIG. 2.45 Polishing cutlery (stage 3)

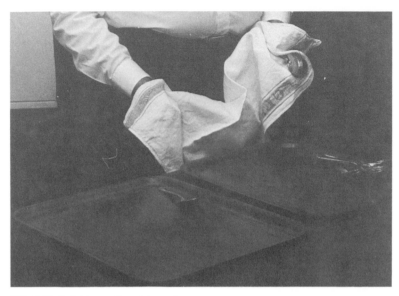

FIG. 2.46 Polishing cutlery (stage 4)

8. Using the thumb of the right hand through the cloth, push out the spoon onto a clean tray, maintaining firm pressure on the handle with thumb and first finger as the spoon is being pushed out, as in Figure 2.46.
9. Repeat for the other pieces of cutlery.

2.3.17 POLISHING GLASSWARE

Glass, by the very nature of the material, is such that any foreign matter on it shows up against light. Any stains or marks inside or outside become very prominent the moment a liquid is poured into it. The easiest way to appreciate this is to pour a coloured fizzy drink, such as orangeade or cola into an unpolished glass. It is for this reason that all glassware must be immaculately cleaned and polished.

Before beginning to polish glasses, one must organise the basic items for the task, as follows:

1. Clear the work surface or table of all items.
2. Collect clean, washed, sorted glasses on a tray.
3. Ensure a supply of clean, lint-free glass cloths sufficient for the job in hand.
4. Place a bowl of boiling water to the left of the glasses to be polished.

FIG. 2.47 Polishing glasses (stage 1)

5. Place a clean tray to the left of the bowl to receive the polished
   glasses. The layout is shown in Figure 2.47.

The skill of polishing glasses is simply that of rubbing all surface
areas (inside and out) with a soft, dry, lint-free cloth, to remove all
foreign matter. A small quantity of moisture helps to loosen any
stains, but too much will increase the friction between glass surfaces
and cloth, making it hard to rub, as well as increasing the risk of
breakage, espcially with thin-sided or fine-stemmed glasses.

Method
1. Hold one corner of the glass cloth in the left hand so that it
   covers the palm and fingers.
2. With the right hand, pick up the nearest glass to be polished
   by holding it from the base of the glass. Check for stains, eg
   lipstick, and also for cracks or chips. Stained glasses should be
   returned for further washing, and damaged glasses should be
   discarded safely.
3. Hold the glass upside-down in the steam escaping from the bowl
   of water, to collect moisture, both inside and outside, as shown
   in Figure 2.48.
4. Transfer the glass to the left hand so that the base of the glass
   is held firmly in the corner of the glass-cloth, as shown in Figure
   2.49.

FIG. 2.48 Polishing glasses (stage 2)

5. With the right-hand thumb push the opposite corner of the glass-cloth into the glass. Push more cloth in so that the cloth reaches the bottom of the glass.

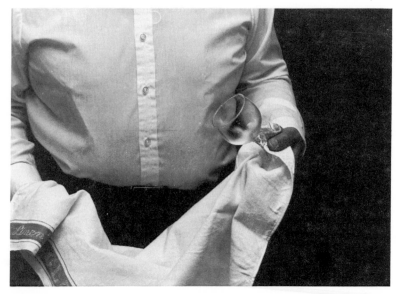

FIG. 2.49 Polishing glasses (stage 3)

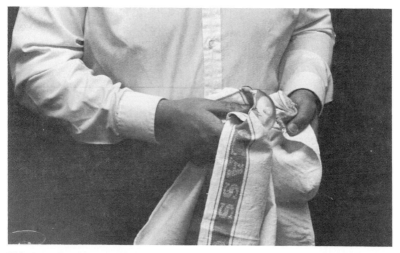

FIG. 2.50 Polishing glasses (stage 4)

6. Hold the glass within the cloth and turn the base of the glass to gently rub the whole of the glass surface, as shown in Figure 2.50.
7. Repeat until the entire surface is rubbed and polished.
8. Remove cloth, still holding the base in the corner of the cloth. Inspect glass against light.

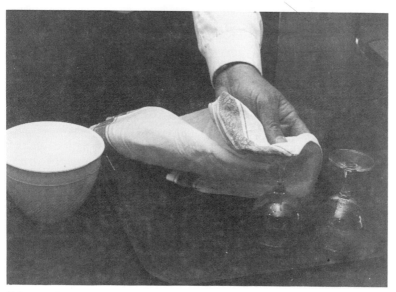

FIG. 2.51 Polishing glasses (stage 5)

9. Place polished glass upside-down on the tray for polished glasses, as shown in Figure 2.51.
10. Repeat from 1 until all glasses necessary have been polished.

2.3.18 POLISHING CROCKERY

Crockery, if properly washed and dried, should not need to be polished. If it shows water marks, then the dish-washer should be checked, because, if operating correctly and with the proper rinsing

FIG. 2.52 (left) Using a waiter's cloth (stage 1)
FIG. 2.53 (right) Using a waiter's cloth (stage 2)

agent added to the detergent, crockery should shine brilliantly, and require no polishing.

If however, due to incorrect washing the crockery is marked, then it should be polished with a clean, dampened glass cloth, finishing off with a dry glass cloth.

2.3.19   USING WAITER'S CLOTH EFFECTIVELY

A waiter's cloth is one of the fundamental tools of the waiter. It

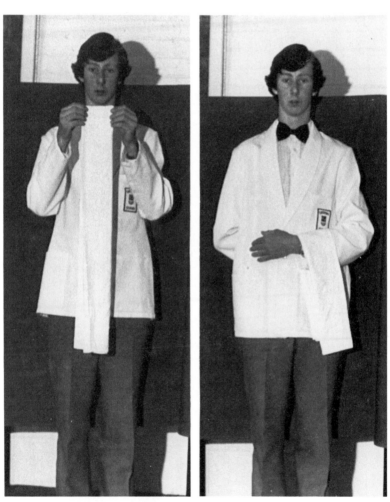

FIG. 2.54 (left) Using a waiter's cloth (stage 3)
FIG. 2.55 (right) Using a waiter's cloth (stage 4)

is therefore essential that a waiter is able to make the best use of this tool in a variety of situations.

Method
1. Check that the waiter's cloth is clean, as in Figure 2.52.
2. Fold in half lengthwise, and again a second time, to give four layers, lengthwise, as in Figures 2.53 and 2.54.
3. Fold the length in half, and hang the cloth from the middle, on the left forearm near the wrist as shown in Figure 2.55. This is the standard position of the cloth and must always be worn

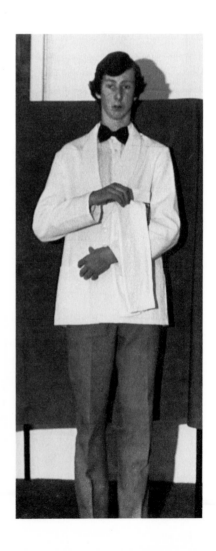

FIGS. 2.56–2.58 (l. to r.) The three stages of making a pad

as such until needed to perform any other task (refer to section 2.3.1, 'Posture at the service sideboard').

4. For the service from large flats, lift off the cloth holding the middle fold between the fingers and thumb of the right hand and sliding out the left arm, as in Figure 2.56.

5. Hold out the left hand and forearm. Place the far ends of the waiter's cloth on the left hand and bring down the folded end near the elbow, thus covering the hand and forearm with eight layers of cloth, providing adequate insulation from a hot service dish, as in Figure 2.57.

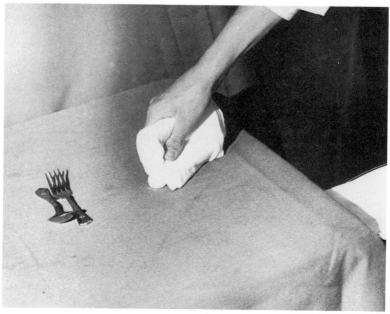

FIG. 2.59 Crumbing-down

6. For smaller service dishes, proceed as in steps 4 and 5 and then fold back the folded end by taking it from the elbow to the hand, thus providing 16 layers of cloth on the palm and part of the forearm, as a tidy pad, as in Figure 2.58.

7. For 'crumbing-down', fold in half two more times and hold securely between fingers and thumb of right hand, giving the effect of holding a 'brush', as shown in Figure 2.59.

8. Use the full length of the cloth when carrying hot plates for service at the table (refer to section 2.3.2, 'Carrying plates').

9. Use half folded for removing hot plates from the hot cupboard. (as in step 4).

10. Use the fold as in step 6 for lifting and moving hot dishes from tray to sideboard etc.

2.3.20 SERVICE POSTURE AT THE TABLE

A waiter is a professional at serving food. The manner of service is as important as the end product of the service itself. One of the most important postures is that which the waiter assumes when actually serving at the table. The correct serving posture not only looks good and professional, it also reduces unnecessary fatigue.

Notes:
1. Before approaching the table, ensure:
   (a) you have adequate quantity of the food to be served.
   (b) the food is adequately hot or cold, as the case may be.
   (c) you know who is to be served with the item.
   (d) you place the dish on your left hand with the waiter's cloth folded in the 'pad' form.
   (e) you carry the serving spoon and fork, if needed, in your right hand.
   (f) that there is an empty hot or cold plate, or a space for the item to be served in front of the diner.
2. Approach the table, to the left of the diner to be served, holding the dish in front of you, but not touching your clothing.
3. Watch out for any item, such as a handbag, etc., under the table, or between the chairs. Place left foot forward near front leg of the diner's chair, and just under the table top.
4. Face the diner you are serving. Look for signs that the diner is aware that you are about to serve. If the diner should move slightly to his right, or makes a gesture that facilitates the service for you, acknowledge this by using a polite expression such as 'thank you'.
5. Bend from the waist, NEVER from the knees, forward, but slightly inclined to your left, as in Figure 2.60.
6. Position your serving dish near to the diner's plate, slightly overlapping if possible, some 10–15 cm above the table.
7. While serving, look for signs from the diner indicating the size of portion that he might wish to have, especially with regard to sauces, gravies and accompaniments. In the absence of any signal from the diner as to the quantity being served, check politely by asking 'would you like some more . . .?', rather than 'is that enough . . .?', before moving to the next diner.

2.3.21 *PLACING PLATES BEFORE DINERS*

Plates, hot for hot food and cold for cold food, should be placed before the diner immediately prior to the service of food items.

Tradition has it that food is served from the left and cleared from the right, based on the facts that for right-handed waiters carrying a flat on their left hand and serving with the right hand this is the obvious and only practical method, and clearing, if carried out with the right hand, permits the plates full of debris to be carried in the waiter's left hand and out of sight of the diners.

Drinks and coffee, on the other hand are served and cleared from the right, this side being more convenient, the diner (being assumed to be right-handed), having drinking glasses, and coffee cups near to his right hand.

The common exceptions to clearing from the right is the clearing of side-plates, which are cleared from the left.

FIG. 2.60 Serving posture at the table

Likewise, as a waiter will be carrying a stack of plates on his left hand, it will be easier for him to place clean plates in front of diners with his right hand, from the right.

There is much controversy over this whole subject with no real consensus of opinion in the matter, and in any case it is subject to house rules, but three factors should be always taken into account; these are:

1. Inconvenience to the diner;
2. Ease of service for the waiter;
3. Safety.

Inconvenience to the diner.   The aim of the waiter should be to cause the least amount of inconvenience to the diner, even if it may cause some difficulty in service. For example, should diners be engrossed in conversation the waiter should use his discretion whether to serve a plated item, such as hors-d'oeuvre from the right rather than interrupt.

Ease of service.   Although the convenience of the diner should always be borne in mind, sometimes it may be necessary to serve or clear from that side which is easier for the waiter in order to enhance the style of service and the presentation of food.

Safety.   Safety, though listed last, must on no account be ignored. If it is not safe to serve from the 'wrong' side, the waiter should be prepared to wait until it is convenient for the diner to be served from the 'correct' side. Only in extreme cases should the diners be inconvenienced by drawing their attention that service needs to be carried out.

When learning to acquire 'food service skills' one must also endeavour to use the correct hand even though one may be used to using their left or right hand in general life in order to minimise any possible inconvenience to diners.

Method
1.*Approach the table with a stack of plates on left hand, the forearm covered with a folded waiter's cloth, as shown in Figure 2.61.
2. Stand behind, slightly to the right-hand side of the diner, with right foot forward.

* Refer to section 2.3.2, 'Carrying a stack of plates'.

FIG. 2.61 Placing plates before diners (stage 1)

FIG. 2.62 Placing plates before diners (stage 2)

FIG. 2.63 Placing plates before diners (stage 3)

FIG. 2.64 Placing plates before diners (stage 4)

3. If the diner has not noticed you, draw his/her attention to you by softly using an expression such as 'sir?' or 'madam?'.
4. Check that there is sufficient clear space on the table for the plate and that there are no obstructions in the way, such as glasses. If necessary, make space for these by moving them out of the immediate area.
5.[†] Using the waiter's cloth, give a gentle, discreet wipe to the top plate. Lift the top plate by inserting slightly spread fingers under the plate and supporting the rim of the plate with the thumb running as near as possible parallel to the edge of the plate, as shown in Figure 2.62.
6.[†] While transferring the plate to the table, keep it slightly tilted so that the view is not obscured by the plate. Rest one edge of the plate on the table and gently lower the rest of the plate, adjusting the position as necessary, as shown in Figures 2.63 and 2.64.

2.3.22 PRESENTATION OF FOOD ON DINER'S PLATES

Attractive presentation of food on the diner's plate enhances the appetite of the diners and shows the professional skills of the waiter. The chefs put in a great deal of effort to decorate the food in the serving dishes, and nothing is worse than a careless waiter ruining that effort when transferring the food from the serving dish to the diner's plate.

The waiter's aims should be (i) to make the food look attractive and appetizing on the plate, and (ii) to make it easier for the diner to mix and eat the items on his plate without having to turn over or 'relocate' those items.

There are no strict rules about how the food should be presented on the plate. However, the following general rules will assist in achieving the above two objectives.

Note: For the purpose of explaining where various items of food should be placed, it helps to consider the plate as the face of a clock, with 12 at the top of the plate and 6 at the bottom of the plate, nearest to the diner.

[†] *Note:*   If a crest or badge of the establishment is printed on the plate, before lifting the plate check that the crest is in the correct position, so that when placed on the table it will be facing the diner.

FIG. 2.65 Presentation of food on diner's plate (drawing)

Method
1. Serve the main item first (ie meat or fish) and place it in the segment between 4 and 8 of the clock face. Any garnishes, other than watercress, should be placed alongside. Cress and watercress should be placed between 11 and 1 of the clockface, as shown in Figure 2.65.
2. Serve the vegetables next, arranging them in neat piles. If the vegetables will require cutting, it is better to place them between the segment of 8 and 12 of the clockface, and others between 12 and 4, NOT forgetting to leave some space for the service of potatoes.
3. Follow the vegetables with potatoes and accommodate them in the gaps left after the service of the vegetables.
4. Serve the sauces and gravies by neatly spooning them over the item to which they belong, or by the side, if preferred by the diner.

Note: Every effort should be made to achieve a symmetrical effect by using the natural shape of the items to advantage. For example, large segments of cauliflower should be arranged to fit neatly into the curve of the plate.

2.3.23 CLEARING PLATES FROM DINERS

Plates should only be cleared from the table when all diners in the party have finished eating the course. Most British diners will indicate this by placing their knives and forks together. If a diner does not indicate that he has finished in this fashion, it may be necessary to wait and observe for a few minutes to ensure that he has. In such cases one should start clearing by approaching that diner and confirm by politely asking before clearing. On no account should any attempt be made to clear the plate without first confirming that it is in order to do so.

As a general rule, the plates should be cleared from the right of the diner. Small tables should be cleared by moving clockwise, and large banqueting tables from right to left, or from the furthest end from the washing-up area.

Method
1. Before clearing, make sure that the diner is aware of your presence.
2. Approach from the right, with right foot forward.
3. Pick up the plate with your right hand, by placing fingers 1 and 2 under the plate and thumb on the rim.
4. Transfer the plate to the left hand, rest it on fingers 1 and 2, thumb on rim, with fingers 3 and 4 crooked upwards to form a platform with the wrist. Make sure that the grip is firm and that the plate is held level.
5. Position the knife blade under the bridge of the fork, so that they make an 'X', as in Figure 2.66.
6. Move to the next diner, position to the right of the diner, with right foot forward and the cleared plate behind the back of the diner. Pick up the next plate.
7. Transfer the plate to the left hand by placing it on the forearm, using the heel of the thumb and the tips of fingers 3 and 4, as in Figure 2.67. Make sure that both plates are kept level.
8. Place the second knife under the fork handle, keeping it parallel to the first knife.
9. Using the fork, scrape any food or debris onto plate 1 as in Figure 2.68 and place the fork parallel and next to fork 1.
10. Repeat as for plate 2, until clearing is completed.
11. Using the right hand, transfer plate 1 onto the top of the stack of plates on the left hand and forearm, and carry the stack to the sideboard.

In the wash-up area the cutlery should be placed in cutlery containers and the debris on the top plate should be put in the bin.

2.3.24   CRUMBING DOWN

At the end of the main course and before the service of the sweet course, it will be necessary to remove from the table any bread

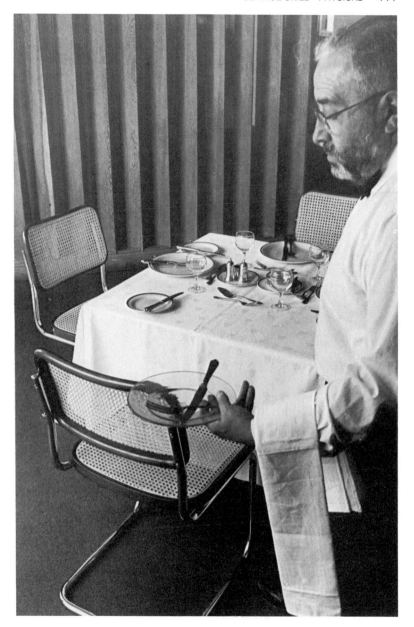

FIG. 2.66 Clearing plates from diners (stage 1, showing grip)

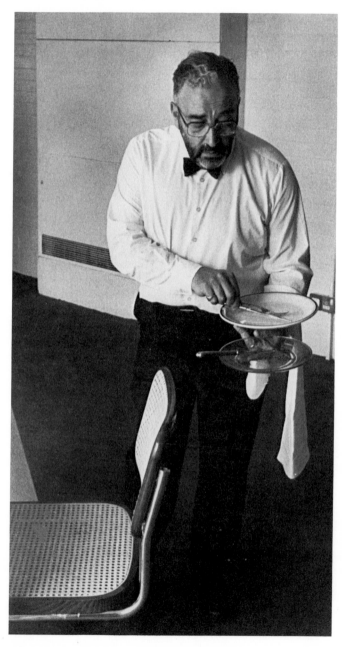

FIG. 2.67 Clearing plates from diners (stage 2)

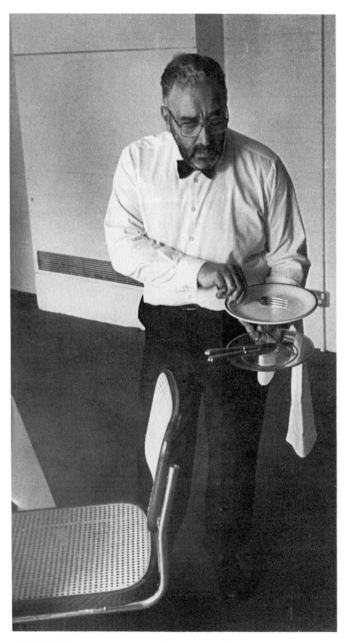

FIG. 2.68 Clearing plates from diners (stage 3)
Clearing plates from diners (stage 4)

crumbs from rolls or Melba toast etc. This is known as 'crumbing down'. At the same time the cover for the sweet course is 'brought down'.

Method

1. Before beginning to crumb down, make sure that all items except the cover for the sweet course (and the ashtray, if the customers are smoking) have been cleared from the table.
2.† Prepare a service plate by lining a joint plate with a paper serviette and fold the waiter's cloth for crumbing down.
3. Approach from the left of the diner, carrying the service plate on the palm of the left hand, folded waiter's cloth in the right. Left foot forward.
4. Bend from the waist. Bring the front edge of the service plate just under the table edge.
5. Using the waiter's cloth, brush down any crumbs onto the service plate, using long gentle strokes, as in Figure 2.69.

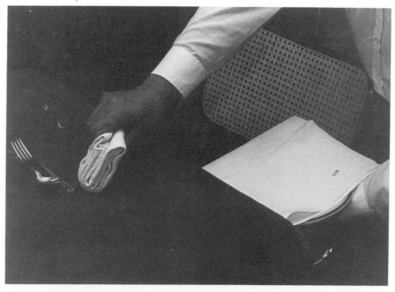

FIG. 2.69 Crumbing down

---

† Some establishments may use small crescent-shaped brushes for crumbing down. Refer to section 2.3.19, 'Using waiter's cloth effectively' for folding the cloth.

6. Place the waiter's cloth on the service plate. Bring down the fork by holding the handle near the prongs between first finger and thumb, and moving it to the left of the 'cover'.
7. Move to the right of the diner, right foot forward and bring down the dessert spoon to the right of the 'cover'.
8. Step back. Approach the next diner on your right (or anti-clockwise), left foot forward.
9. Continue until crumbing down is completed for all diners.

2.3.25   PRESENTING AND CHANGING ASHTRAYS

As a general rule, ashtrays are not placed on the table at the beginning of the service. However, if diners are smoking, or begin to smoke before the service of the first course, a clean ashtray should be placed on the table. It is important that the ashtray be removed just before or just after the first course is served.

If the diners are smoking after the meal the ashtray should be left on the table, and periodically changed, if necessary. Tables with more than four covers will require more than one ashtray.

Method
1. Collect a clean ashtray and place it upside down on a salver or service plate lined with a serviette.

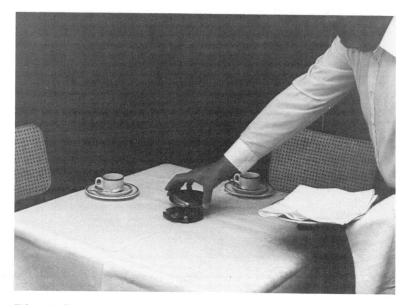

FIG. 2.70 Changing ashtrays (stage 1)

FIG. 2.71 Changing ashtrays (stage 2)

FIG. 2.72 Changing ashtrays (stage 3)

2. Approach the table from the side which will cause least inconvenience to the diners.

3. Cover the dirty ashtray with the clean ashtray placed upside-down on it, as in Figure 2.70.

4. Keeping the dirty ashtray covered, remove both ashtrays together and place them on the salver. This will prevent any ash from flying about, as in Figure 2.71.

5. Replace the clean ashtray on the table, if required, as in Figure 2.72.

3

RESTAURANT TASKS

3.1 PRE-SERVICE TASKS (MISE EN PLACE)

3.1.1 CLEANING DUTIES (MÉNAGE)

Normal day-to-day cleaning of the 'room' (as the restaurant is usually called) is mainly carried out by the waiting staff, covering all items, but periodic 'heavy' cleaning may be carried out by either maintenance staff (in a hotel) or outside contractors, and this work will usually be carried out either at night, or during a closure for decoration purposes.

The daily cleaning procedures will be designated by the head waiter responsible for the room and staff will be delegated various tasks on a rota basis depending on the frequency of repetition of these tasks, which are as follows: Furniture; Floor surfaces; Wall coverings; Curtains; Metalwork and mirrors etc.

3.1.1.1. Furniture

Will normally consist of tables, sideboards, chairs, banquette seating or fixed counters, and treatment will depend on the type of finish, as follows:

Polished wood. A good general purpose furniture cream, either liquid or aerosol may be used, with a clean soft duster. Should the items be greasy from frequent handling, such as sideboards or the backs of chairs, they should be cleaned with hot water to which some vinegar has been added before drying and polishing. If the surface is resin-sealed then it can be cleaned with hot water to which some detergent has been added.

Great care must be taken with furniture that has been french polished that it does not come into contact with methylated spirits if spirit-fuelled flare lamps are used, because the spirit will remove the polish, which will necessitate costly re-polishing.

Melamine or resin-finished furniture covered with simulated wood finishes such as Formica are normally cleaned (if soiled) using a detergent solution with a spray polish to finish.

Chairs with wood frames should be polished as above. If fabric-covered the covers should be brushed before the frames are dusted or polished. Imitation leather covers should be polished using a suitable aerosol polish, or following the instructions of the manufacturers of the fabric.

Note: It is best to polish chair stiles, legs and arms by spraying polish onto a cloth to avoid overspray onto upholstery.

3.1.1.2 Floor surfaces

Carpets. Maintenance of these will depend on the actual surface used. Most luxury-type restaurants will have a carpeted floor which gives a rich effect to the room when laid-up ready for opening.

In normal use, carpets should be cleaned using a vacuum cleaner during the 'mise en place' period when all chairs can be placed on the tables (unless polished) to make cleaning easier, and to reveal the whole floor surface. Should the vacuum cleaner used not permit cleaning to the edges, a stiff brush should be used to remove crumbs or fluff from the edges of the room before vacuuming is carried out.

Between lunch and dinner services, a carpet sweeper is often used to remove visible crumbs because the room may already be laid up and clothed.

If any spills involving foodstuffs occur, they should be mopped up immediately and washed using warm, soapy water, having first removed as much solid or semi-solid matter as possible.

Should the carpet be badly stained, then shampooing techniques should be employed, either during the night closure, or during annual closure.

Parquet flooring. This is not often seen now in restaurants, except perhaps those with a dance floor. Treatment should be as follows.

The floor should first be swept using a soft brush or vacuum cleaner to remove all dust and debris, such as cigarette ends. If available, a floor-polishing machine should then be used, otherwise a polish applicator followed by a rotary buffer. The polish used will depend on the original treatment of the floor; whether it is wax-finished, or treated with polyurethane varnish.

Thermoplastic tiles. These tiles, such as Marleytiles, Accoflex etc should only be cleaned following the instructions supplied by the manufacturer, because some should be treated with water-based polishes, and others with spirit-based polishes.

Various firms supply different types of cleaning and polishing materials for these floors and offer an advisory service to users on their the best treatment.

Though very easy to clean and polish they are found, generally, in fast-food operations and institutional situations. Care must be taken to clean well round fixed furniture items to avoid black, greasy rings which will require special labour-intensive treatment.

3.1.1.3 Wall coverings

Several types of wall covering may be found in restaurants, as follows: Wallpapers, flock and relief; Hessian; Stone – rustic or polished; Tiled or Vitrolite (opaque coloured glass); Painted.

Methods of cleaning vary according to the materials used and whether one considers daily or seasonal needs.

Wallpapers – flock and relief. These should be vacuumed at least once a week to remove accumulated dust. If soiled badly, relief papers may be washed (if painted over) or sealed and painted over. Flock papers, if really badly soiled, must be stripped and replaced.

Hessian. The only treatment necessary for these is to be vacuumed regularly in order to remove accumulated dust. They can be further protected in certain places (eg next to table-tops) by having glass panels screwed on to them.

Stone. Rustic. Regular vacuum cleaning is all that is necessary for keeping rough stone walls in good order.

Polished. Washing down with detergent solution or other cleaner, if soiled, followed by a spray polish.

Tiles or Vitrolite. As for polished stone (above).

Painted walls. Washing down if soiled will be effective, using a proprietary product. If discoloured, re-painting will be necessary.

3.1.1.4 Curtains

If restaurants have heavy drapes, these must be vacuumed regularly, especially in folds, to remove dust. Periodically they must be sent to be cleaned, and unless such cleaning is carried out during annual closure, a second set should be at hand.

Light-weight curtains (lined or unlined) may be laundered, in which case it is essential to have a replacement set.

Net curtains also must be kept regularly washed because they attract both dust and nicotine stains, and if not clean will look unattractive.

3.1.1.5   *Metalwork, mirrors*

Metalwork to be found in restaurants can be of several types, such as: Chromium-plated; Brass – natural or lacquered; Stainless steel; Wrought iron; Anodised aluminium.

The general treatment for all of these with the exception of natural brass and wrought iron is the same. An aerosol polish and duster normally will be sufficient to keep them bright in daily use.

Wrought iron should be dry dusted and natural brass should be cleaned, using a proprietary brass polish. On no account should one attempt to polish lacquered brass using brass polish.

Mirrors should be cleaned using either a product such as Windolene or other purpose-made spray, finishing with a dry clean lint-free cloth. Should they be neglected, they can be cleaned with warm water containing a little ammonia.

Windows can be cleaned using the same materials as for mirrors, although in many restaurants window cleaning is often contracted to professionals.

3.1.2   CARRYING AND ARRANGING FURNITURE

In restaurants in which all furniture is free-standing (ie neither bolted down as in fast-food outlets, nor pew type or banquette seating arrangements) it is often necessary to move chairs and tables either for ease of cleaning or to re-arrange the room to accommodate special parties.

Care must always be taken in moving any articles of furniture so as not to cause damage to the items being moved or to the decor. Possibly, of more importance from the requirements of the Health and Safety at Work Act 1974, moving furniture should not injure anyone, and one must, therefore work within one's own physical capabilities and not incur any strain.

Should the weight of the items and the headroom permit, it has long been the practice in restaurants to carry both chairs and tables (small) above the head with the legs uppermost, allowing a clear view all round.

Arrangement of furniture in a restaurant is a topic area on which there is always much discussion possible, but the keynote should always be SYMMETRY. In a large, long restaurant, nothing looks worse than the tables being arranged in a haphazard way.

Space must always be allowed for the free passage of waiting staff between tables and also for the passage of trollies. Allowance must be made in deciding widths of gangways for seated diners, dependent on the width of trollies used.

It is important also not to have diners sitting in positions where there may be draughts from an open entrance door, or too near to service doors where they might be annoyed by the noise of service staff going to or from the kitchens etc.

In arranging tables, it must be borne in mind that diners usually like to look into the room, and if space permits, tables for two covers should be placed so that the corner of the table is nearest to the wall and the diners seated at adjacent sides, facing into the room.

3.1.3 USING A TROLLEY: MANOEUVRING, PUSHING

Trollies of various sizes are often used in restaurants. They fall into two categories, those used for service and those used for transport.

Under the service category fall hors-d'oeuvre, sweet, cheese, liqueur, carving the flambé trollies. Under the transport heading are those which may be used during the mise en place period to transport crockery, cutlery, and glassware into the restaurant.

Most trollies have rubber-tyred castors at each corner which permit steering. With the exception of negotiating door thresholds or carpet strips, when trollies must be pulled in order not to lose the load, trollies must always be pushed as a safe working practice, in order not to damage furniture or inconvenience diners or colleagues.

In siting trollies during service, they should always be manoeuvred so that the contents of the trolley may be clearly seen by the diner, and the service staff should be behind the trolley or to one side, in order to help the diner with his choice.

Sufficient plates and clean service cutlery should always be available on the trolley.

The size of any cloths used on a trolley should not be so that they risk catching in the castors.

Notes:
General
1. Most trollies have four swivelling castors, but some have two swivelling castors and two fixed wheels.
2. Load the trolley so that the weight of items on it is evenly distributed so far as possible.
3. Stack items securely. Similar items of crockery should be stacked

together. Avoid stacking glassware and carrying bottles.

4. If the items on the trolley are likely to slip, line the trolley top with an appropriate sized cloth (or a used table cloth, suitably folded).

5. Always push the trolley forwards so that you can keep an eye on the items being carried while you steer to your destination.

6. When steering through doors (swing-or push-through), stop the trolley with the front edge about 450 mm (18 in) short of the door. Go to the front of the trolley, then pull the trolley in with you, as you gently push open the door with your back. Ensure that the entire length of the trolley is clear of the path of the swing of the door before releasing the door.

Notes:
Manoeuvring

1. To steer a trolley in a straight line, exert equal pressure forward on both sides of the rear end of the trolley. Control the direction of the trolley by decreasing pressure on the side towards which you would like the trolley to move. This controls the direction of the swivel of the front wheels, the rear wheels then follow.

2. Sometimes it may be necessary to manoeuvre the rear wheels, for turning round sharp corners, or around tables in the restaurant. This can be achieved by applying pressure from the side of the trolley at the end which needs to be moved. This will have the effect of moving the trolley on three wheels, pivoted on one of the front wheels, depending on the direction in which it is being pushed. (The front wheel of the side that you are pushing acts as a pivot.)

3. When it may be necessary to turn the trolley around by 180 degrees, for example to present to the diner a dish which is on the far side, this may be achieved by holding the trolley from two opposite corners (diagonally) and applying pressure at each end in the opposite direction. This will have the effect of turning the trolley like a turntable, as if the trolley was pivoted in the centre.

Note: The best method to learn these skills is by applying the above three rules to a trolley and observing the movement of the trolley.

3.1.4 CLOTHING TABLES: RESTAURANT AND BANQUETING

There are three main reasons for covering tables with table-cloths:
1. To improve the appearance and presentation.

2. To soften any noise made while placing items of crockery and cutlery.
3. To minimise the movement of plates and other items while diners are eating their meals.

Table-cloths should be laid with the minimum possible handling to keep their laundry-fresh crisp look.

Notes:
  1. Before laying a table cloth, check that the table is steady by gently trying to rock it from diagonal ends. If not steady, insert a piece of cork or folded menu under one leg.
  2. Check the table surface for any loose dust and check with the hand for any dampness which would stain or soil the table-cloth.
  3.*Select a correct size table-cloth. Learn to feel for the weight of the table-cloth. With experience it should be possible to select the correct size by feeling the weight.
  4. Stand at the table centrally between the legs. For oblong tables stand by the longer side.
  5. Place the folded cloth on the table so that the folded ends are on the top and facing the right-hand side.
  6. Place the right-hand side of the folded table-cloth in line with the centre of the table, as in Figure 3.1.

FIG. 3.1 Clothing tables (stage 1)

* Refer to section 2.2.11, Identifying restaurant linen for correct sizes of table-cloth.

FIG. 3.2 Clothing tables (stage 2)

FIG. 3.3 Clothing tables (stage 3)

7.*Using the left hand, unfold the top fold, and using the right hand unfold the second fold. The table-cloth should now hang

* Depending on how the table-cloth is folded, it may be necessary to turn the table-cloth over. Also in case of screen fold, the centre fold will be in the middle. In that case follow the same procedure, except that in step 12 the middle fold will be released from between the middle and forefingers.

equally on either side of the table. Check that the centre fold is on the top and single ends underneath, as shown in Figures 3.2 and 3.3.

8. Keeping a suitable gap between the two hands, hold the centre fold between the thumbs and forefingers, as shown in Figure 3.4.

9. Still holding the centre fold, lift and hold the next single end of the table-cloth between middle and first fingers, as shown in Figure 3.5.

10. Lift off the table-cloth leaving the bottom most end hanging loose.

11. Bend from the waist to reach the far end of the table and allow the loose end to drop behind the far end, as shown in Figure 3.6.

12. Rest the table-cloth on the table and release the middle fold from between the thumbs and forefingers while still holding the single end between middle and forefingers.

13. Pull back the single fold, with a slight shake if necessary. Straighten up as you pull back, bringing the single fold over the near side, as shown in Figure 3.7.

FIG. 3.4 Clothing tables (stage 4)

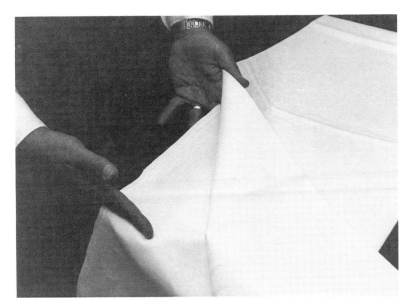

FIG. 3.5 Clothing tables (stage 5)

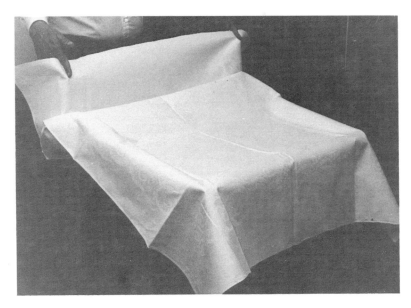

FIG. 3.6 Clothing tables (stage 6)

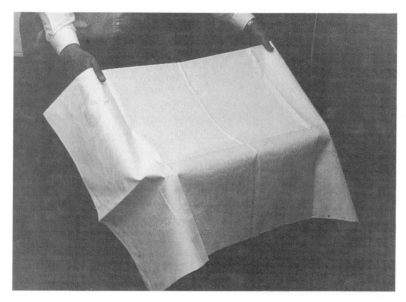

FIG. 3.7 Clothing tables (stage 7)

FIG. 3.8 Clothing tables (stage 8)

14.*Check that the drop is equal on all sides, as shown in Figure 3.8. Adjust if necessary by gently pulling the cloth in the required direction by the selvedge or hem, and NOT by the edge where it falls from the table, as this causes creases and fingermarks.

Notes: Banqueting tables are long tables, and the clothing of them is therefore best achieved by working in pairs. Most good establishments will keep in stock suitable length cloths to cover the different length tables.

Sometimes, however, it is necessary to overlap two smaller length cloths to cover a long table.

Method:
1. Select a correct size table cloth for the table. (Approximately 450–600 mm longer than the table.)
2. Lay the cloth at one end of the table, with the open ends facing the edge of the table.
3. Unfold the cloth until the cloth is laid in the centre of the table, lengthwise.
4. With one person at each end, unfold the cloth and hold it taut.
5. Gently lower the cloth on to the table, making sure that the cloth hangs equally on all sides of the table. (As a general guide, the centre crease of the cloth should run along the centre line of the table, with the crease uppermost.)

3.1.5 LAYING-UP OF TABLE: STANDARD AND NON-STANDARD

The aim of laying-up a table before the service of the meal is to minimise the need for bringing or changing pieces of cutlery and equipment during the meal itself. Thus the table lay-up will be determined by the type of menu/meal being served and the practice in individual establishments.

The procedure is similar for each type of lay-up, and illustrations of different types of table lay-ups are shown in Figures 3.9 to 3.12.

A table d'hôte lay-up will normally consist of sufficient cutlery to cover all the courses offered on the menu.

An à la carte cover will normally consist of a 'show-plate', a serviette, a fish cover, side plate with side knife, and wine glass/es.

* A little practice should eliminate the need for adjusting the drop.

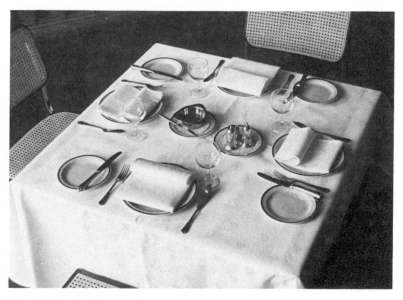

FIG. 3.9 Standard lay-up – À la carte

FIG. 3.10 Standard lay-up – Table d'Hôte

FIG. 3.11 Standard lay-up – Breakfast

Method
1. Check that all tables have been clothed and the chairs are in position before laying-up.
2. Take a stack of side-plates and place a side-plate for each cover in the middle of the cover. This forms the basis for each cover.
3. Pick up a handful of joint knives covered with a clean glass cloth.
4. As you lay-up, give a final polish to each piece and place on the table holding the item from the middle between first finger and thumb. Never touch the blades, prongs or bowls of spoons.

FIG. 3.12 Standard lay-up – Afternoon Tea

5.*Repeat steps 3 and 4 for each item of cutlery required (except side-knives), placing them in the position required.

6. When all items have been placed, inspect and adjust covers for neatness and symmetry.

7. Move side-plate to the left of the cover and place a side-knife on the side-plate. Repeat for each cover.

8. Place a cruet set in the middle of the table. (Tables of more than four covers will require additional cruet sets, conveniently placed.)

9. Place additional pieces of equipment as per the practice of the establishment.

Note: In the opinion of the authors: 1. It is unnecessary to place a table number on the table. 2. Butter in butter dish should only be brought to the table after the guests have been seated.

3.1.6 FOLDING SERVIETTES

Although still practised in many restaurants at home and abroad, the once common art of folding serviettes or table-napkins is now

---

* Suggested order for laying-up a 'table d'hôte' cover: joint knife, joint fork, fish knife, fish fork, soup spoon, dessert fork, dessert spoon, wine glass/es, serviette.

felt out-of-place on hygienic grounds that diners do not wish to feel that an item placed to the mouth has been over-handled before use, apart from the fact that it is a labour-intensive activity with no return for the restaurant.

Certain folds however have their place on buffets and for festive occasions, and so a selection of the more common ones is given, although the authors feel that the Swiss or German style, with the top fold of the laundered serviette turned under without being pressed down is probably an acceptable simple style which can be placed using a spoon and fork. The French method of placing a laundered serviette squarely onto the 'show-plate' of a cover is considered rather stark in Britain.

In order to achieve a properly-folded serviette it is essential to have it well-starched by the laundry. For the French method, it must be folded twice, as shown in figure 3.13. For the Swiss fold, it must be folded three times, as shown in Figure 3.13; this fold also being the basis for the Cone or Dunce's Cap.

Should it be felt necessary in general use to have a folded serviette, then 'Cone' or 'Dunce's Cap' can be done with little handling.

The 'Rose' is very useful as a container for small round dishes, melba toast etc, and for table d'hôte or breakfast situations using smaller or paper serviettes, then the serviette folded into a triangle and placed on the bread-plate is acceptable.

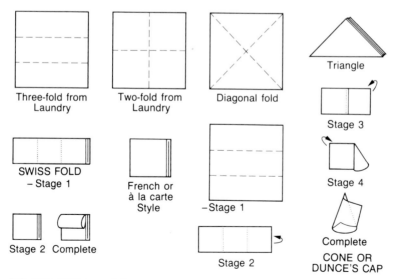

FIG. 3.13 Folding serviettes

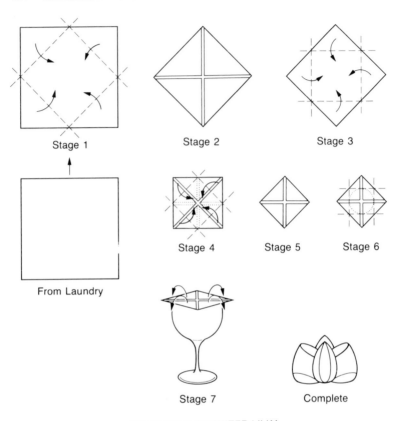

Stage 1

From Laundry

Stage 2

Stage 3

Stage 4

Stage 5

Stage 6

Stage 7

Complete

ROSE-FOLD OR WATER-LILLY

FIG. 3.14(a) Folding serviettes

The number of different folds is endless, with over 100 being shown in a seventeenth-century French work called 'The Maître d'Hôtel'. Several modern works have been published on the subject, one of the most recent being *The Art of Napkin Folding*, James Ginders, Northwood *1978*.

Method
Stages refer to Figure 3.13 and 3.14.

Cone or Dunce's Cap
1. Take a flat serviette, shiny side down. (Stage 1).
2. Turn up the edge nearest you to one-third of the height.
3. Turn down the edge furthest from you over the other to the first fold made. (Stage 2).

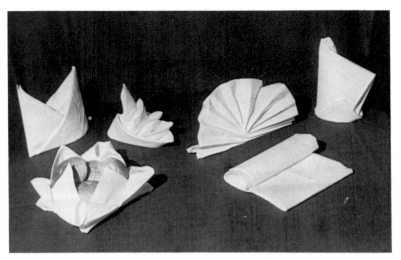

FIG. 3.14(b) Folded serviettes   *Back row* (l. to r.): Bishop's mitre; Cockscomb; Fan; Cone or Dunce's cap   *Front row* (l. to r.): Rose-fold or water-lily; Swiss fold

4. Turn the right-hand edge towards the left to a position of two-thirds of the length. (Stage 3).
5. Roll the top right-hand corner down with the right hand inside. (Stage 4).
6. Bring top left-hand corner down to coincide with the point of the roll.
7. Remove hand from inside roll, holding both points together, and ensuring that there is no gap at the top, turn up the two points to give a level base.

Rose-fold or Water-lily
1. Starting with a flat serviette, shiny side down, turn all four corners into the centre as shown in Stage 2.
2. With the smaller square that you now have, repeat the procedure twice more. (Stages 3 to 6).
3. Holding the folds tight, place the serviette, flat side down over a Paris goblet, and while holding it down onto the glass, pull out and down the eight points. (Stage 7).
4. Adjust to resemble a rose or water-lily.

3.1.7 FILLING CRUETS

Before the beginning of each service it is essential to ensure that all cruets are adequately filled. This task is usually carried out during the morning 'mise en place' period but checking should be carried out in any case during the afternoon closure.

Waiting staff must get to know the type of cruets used in the establishment eg are they of screw-type or push-together type? Most catering establishments nowadays select cruet design to permit refilling without inversion which makes for ease of work and reduces mess.

Method
1. Collect ALL cruets in the restaurant onto a medium-sized tray, keeping salt to one side and pepper to the other.
2. Select a suitable work-surface in a draught-free and well-illuminated area of the restaurant or the pantry.
3. Collect salt, pepper and a clean glass/polishing cloth together with a teaspoon or coffee spoon, another medium-sized tray and some cocktail sticks or paper pins.
4. Unscrew/open the tops of all of the same type (either salt or pepper) inspecting for any blocked holes in the caps and keeping separate those needing cleaning or attention.
5. Retain the bases on the tray neatly arranged in rows.
6. Using tea-coffee-spoon refill the bases about 3/4 full.
7. Attend to the caps, unblocking holes as necessary using cocktail stick/pin etc.
8. Replace caps on bases.
9. Using the polishing cloth, wipe clean the outside of the cruet and place the finished cruets on to the clean tray.
10. Repeat the above procedure for other condiment.

Note:
1. For one-piece cruets with a rubber/nylon stopper in the base, it will be necessary to invert the cruet to remove the stopper and refill. In this case, refill one at a time and replace the stopper, as follows: block the holes with the palm of the left hand, before inverting, filling and replacing the stopper.
2. Before proceeding to refill the second condiment it is essential that all caps have been replaced on the first ones to avoid mixing of the caps which results in the embarrassing situation of diners sprinkling pepper on their food instead of salt.
3. Periodically (usually once per week) all cruets should be emptied, polished, washed, thoroughly dried and rubbed up with a dry, soft cloth before refilling.

3.1.8 MAKING MUSTARD

English mustard should always be freshly made for each meal unless proprietary prepared English mustard is used in the establishment. Other proprietary mustards (French, German etc) should also be made available, should diners require them.

Method
1. Collect mustard and equipment to make mustard, ie a container large enough in which to mix the required quantity, a mixing spoon, a small container of fresh water, and clean mustard pots.
2. Using the dry mixing spoon, measure out into the mixing container sufficient quantity of mustard to be prepared.
3. Add a small quantity of water at a time, and keep mixing the mustard with the mixing spoon until the consistency of a thick paste is reached.
4. Using a teaspoon or coffee-spoon, spoon the prepared mustard into the mustard pots.
5. Wipe clean the outside of the pots and the rim.

Note: After the mustard has been left to stand for a while, a layer of water appearing on the surface indicates that too much water had been added. In such a case, before presenting the mustard to the guest, the waiter should give it a gentle stir, so that the water is absorbed back into the mustard.

3.1.9 PREPARING AND CLOTHING SIDEBOARDS: CLOTHING AND EQUIPPING

A sideboard is the base from which waiting staff operates. It should therefore carry all the equipment that a waiter is likely to need during the service of a meal. The size and design of the sideboard will depend on the type of menu and the number of covers to be served from each sideboard.

The arrangement of equipment will vary from one establishment to another. It is, however, recommended that each establishment should have a standard lay-up to ease service and promote flexibility in staffing. The following factors should be taken into account:
1. Items required frequently should be placed so as to minimise bending.
2. Heavier items such as plates should be placed on the lower shelf.
3. Cutlery items in the drawers should be arranged in such an order that similar items are not kept in adjacent compartments, eg

joint knives and side knives should be separated by placing joint forks in between.

4. Work-top of the sideboard to be kept clear of all items at all times.

5. Overall appearance of the arrangement should be neat, tidy and aesthetic.

Note: Older-type sideboards that are not supplied with plasticised surfaces should have their shelves covered with sideboard cloths, their front edges folded under. (Sideboard cloths are usually made from old table-cloths).

Method

1. Clear sideboard of all items.
2. Remove the cutlery drawers and clean them out, turning upside-down if necessary and brushing out, if felted.
3. Line drawers with clean folded paper serviettes. (This is not necessary if the drawers are felt-lined).
4. Wipe all surfaces and sides with a damp cloth.
5. Cloth lower shelves, if necessary.
6. Check each item for cleanliness before placing in the sideboard.
    Suggested order for placing items in sideboard is shown as Figure 3.15, will depend on the number of shelves:

Top: Clear.

Drawers: Cutlery items: knives, forks, spoons etc. (handles outwards).

Shelf 1:   Crockery items: joint plates, fish-plates, side-plates, saucers.

Shelf 2:   Cruets, sugar dredger, oil and vinegar, proprietary sauces, mustards, water jug, spare glasses, roll basket.

Shelf 3:   Salvers, service plate, ashtrays, spare serviettes.

3.1.10 PREPARING FLARE LAMPS

Flare lamps, of varying external styles, are of three main types:

Propane or butane gas.   Either with internal replaceable cylinders, or if fitted in a trolley, piped to a gas cylinder such as Calor or another brand.

Methylated spirit.   These can be either: adjustable, wicked type, or vapourising type which have a snuffer or cover to adjust the flame.

FIG. 3.15 Preparation of sideboard

Prior to service the outside surface of the lamp must be cleaned, according to the type of metal from which it is made. The top grid, if steel, should be cleaned with a nylon scourer, or steel wool, to remove blackening, burnt-on grease, or food particles.

After cleaning the gas-type lamp it is only necessary to check that the gas cylinder is not empty and that the jets are not blocked.

The methylated-spirit-fuelled lamp must be refilled. The adjustable wicked-type usually has a filler-cap on the side of the base tank, and must be filled using a funnel. A check must be made that there is sufficient wick and that the adjuster works freely. The vapourising type is usually filled through the hole in the top. Any spilt spirit should be wiped off with a damp cloth as it often becomes sticky when dry. Care must be taken when filling with spirit that it does not come into contact with polished wooden surfaces, because it removes french polish, or any shellac-based polishes.

3.1.11   CLEANING AND REFILLING PROPRIETARY SAUCE BOTTLES

Proprietary sauce bottles when presented to the diner should be at least three-quarters full. It is for this reason that sauce bottles are filled at the end of each service. Alternatively, the task may be performed before the service of the meal.

Method
1. On a medium-sized tray, collect the sauce bottles, segregating the different kinds.
2. Collect a damp cloth, a dry cloth, and a bowl of hand-hot water.
3. For sauces such as ketchup, keep the cap on and stand the bottle upside-down, so that the remaining sauce collects in the neck of the bottle.
4. *Bottles less than half-full of sauce should be emptied into bottles which are more than half-full.
5. Once the bottles have been refilled, clean the outside of the bottles with the damp cloth.
6. Using one end of the damp cloth, clean the inside of the neck of the bottle.
7. Wash the caps in the bowl of warm water, and dry with the dry cloth.
8. Replace caps on bottles and clear the empties away.
9. Store the refilled bottles upright.

3.1.12   PREPARING BREAD, ROLLS AND TOAST FOR SERVICE

Bread.   Using a sharp knife remove crusts from all sides of the slices. Cut diagonally in half. Arrange neatly with slices overlapping in a bread-boat lined with a paper serviette.

Rolls.   Arrange rolls neatly, right side up in a serviette-lined bread-boat.

Toast   (for breakfast). Using thick-sliced bread, after toasting, cut diagonally into half and place in a toast rack. Present the toast in the rack on a suitable underplate.

Toast   (for lunch or dinner). Using thin-sliced bread, after toasting on both sides, use a sharp knife to remove crusts from all sides. Cut diagonally into half. Arrange neatly in a bread-boat lined with a paper serviette, slices overlapping, or if to be served hot, for use with paté, in a linen serviette folded into a 'pocket' placed on a suitable-sized plate.

* To facilitate the pouring of sauce from one bottle to another a special screwed adaptor is available on the market.

Melba toast. Using thick-sliced bread toast on both sides. Using a sharp knife remove the crusts from all sides, then slice the toast into half its thickness. Toast again the untoasted sides of the halves. Arrange on a suitably-sized plate, lined with a serviette, or in a 'rose' folded serviette.

3.1.13 PREPARING BUTTER FOR SERVICE

Butter is normally prepared before the service in the still-room using one of several methods according to house custom.

The main aim is to render the butter into manageable portions. The methods usually employed are as follows: Butter pats (using a machine); Butter curls; Butter blocks; Butter in pads.

Butter pats. (Using a butter-pat machine, as in Figure 3.16)
1. Take butter from the fridge and insert blocks of butter into the cylinder provided, making sure, as far as possible, that the cylinder is firmly filled, excluding as much air as possible.
2. Place the piston in position and assemble the cylinder onto the machine.
3. Adjust the lever for the thickness of pat required.
4. Place a bowl of iced water under the cutting wire of the machine.
5. Turn the handle and collect the pats in the iced water.

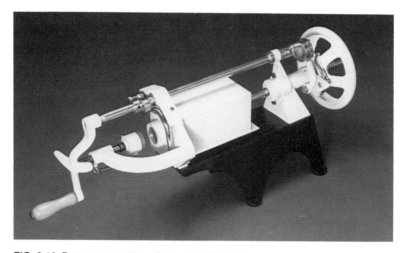

FIG. 3.16 Butter-pat machine (Buttapatta Co Ltd)

Butter curls.
1. Allow the butter to stand for 5–10 minutes after taking it out of the fridge.
2. Collect butter-curling tool, jug of hot water and bowl of cold water with ice.
3. Dip the curling tool into the hot water, then draw across the surface of the butter, curling the top layer into suitable-sized curls.
4. Place the curl into the iced water.
5. Continue with the rest of the butter, dipping the tool into the hot water between each curling.

Butter blocks.
1. Collect butter from the fridge, a sharp knife, a jug of very hot water, and a bowl of cold water with ice.
2. Unwrap and mark the block of butter for the size of block required. (A block of 250g can be divided into 32 pats by marking the block to be cut into two halves through the thickness, marking each half down the centre of the length, then marking each length into 8.)
3. Dip the knife into the hot water, allowing it to warm up.
4. Cut the butter on the marked lines, dipping the knife into the hot water between each cutting.
5. Place the cut blocks into the iced water.

Note:
1. Because of body heat causing partial melting, and from hygienic considerations, butter should never be handled. A fork *must* always be used.
2. Butter prepared by any of the above methods is then arranged in a butter dish for each order and decorated with a sprig of parsley.

Butter pads.   These are small, varying sized earthenware dishes into which butter is placed and scraped level with the top surface. One is served as a portion to each diner or a table.

3.1.14   PREPARING SUNDRIES FOR SERVICE: WATER JUGS, FINGER BOWLS AND LEMON

Preparing water jugs
1. Select clean water jugs. Check that they are not chipped or cracked.

2. Fill the jugs two-thirds full with cold freshly-drawn drinking water.
3. Add a few ice cubes and a slice of lemon.
4. Place the jugs on sideboards on a suitable sized underplate lined with a folded linen serviette. (Paper serviette will soak up any condensation that will drip down the side of the jug and disintegrate.)

Preparing finger bowls
Finger bowls are part of the cover for any dish for which the diner may need to use his fingers for eating (eg globe artichokes). Whenever a finger bowl is placed with the cover, a small spare serviette should also accompany.
1. Collect clean finger bowls.
2. Half-fill with luke-warm water.
3. Add a slice of lemon.
4. Place the finger bowl on a side-plate with doily slightly to the right of the diner, or to the left, whichever is more convenient.

Preparing lemon
Lemon is used in the restaurant for several purposes and is usually prepared in two fashions, either segments, or sliced. Both methods start in the same way.
1. Take a sharp stainless knife and cutting board.
2. Place lemon on board and cut off both ends to give a flat end surface.
3. Cut the lemon in two halves down its length.

For Slices. Place the half lemon, cut-side down on the board, and slice across with the knife to the thickness required, removing any pips.

For Segments. Place the half lemon on its end on the board and cut down into segments of the required size, removing any pips while doing so.

Cut lemon should be stored either in lemon juice or slightly salted water in order to prevent it drying out.

3.1.15 PREPARING GLASSES FOR SERVICE

Before the service, sufficient glasses for use in the restaurant must be cleaned and polished (see also section 2. 3.17).

3.1.15.1 Choosing glasses

This will depend on house custom. Most restaurants will lay-up covers with a general-purpose wine glass such as a 6 2/3 oz. Paris goblet, but others will lay-up both a Paris goblet and a white wine flute.

For special functions, or parties where a set menu and pre-chosen wines have been ordered, it is in order, and common practice to lay-

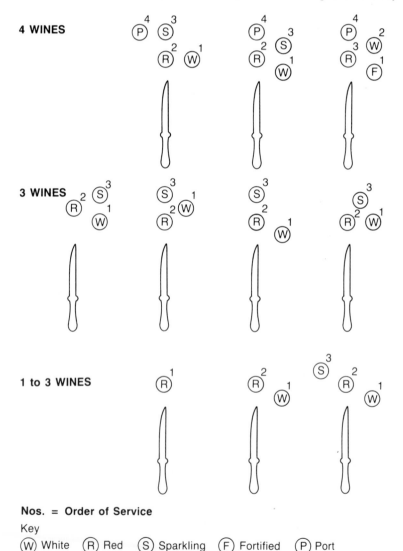

Nos. = Order of Service

Key

(W) White   (R) Red   (S) Sparkling   (F) Fortified   (P) Port

FIG. 3.17 Placing of glasses

up sufficient glasses for all wines to be served during the meal.

3.1.15.2   Placing glasses

When one is placed on the table, it is centred on the tip of the joint knife. When two glasses are laid, then the red-wine glass goes at the tip of the joint knife, with the white-wine glass slightly in front and to the right.

For situations where more glasses are to be laid, the layout is shown in Figure 3.17.

3.1.16   PREPARATION AND MAINTENANCE OF TABLE FLOWER VASES

Flowers on restaurant tables help to improve décor and ambience, but two points must be considered:
1. Vases and flowers should not be so large as to impede conversation between diners, nor to impede the service in any way.
2. They should always be kept well tended in order to avoid smells caused by rotting leaves, etc.

Vases for restaurant tables fall into two main types, tall and slim for one or two longer-stemmed blooms; or bowls or posy-rings for flower heads. Both types can be made from either metal, glass or china.

Flowers should be checked daily and any that are no longer fresh discarded. The stems of soft-stemmed flowers should be re-cut and hard-stemmed flowers such as roses, carnations or chrysanthemums should be hammered or crushed. Water should be topped up and

FIG. 3.18 Restaurant flower vases

FIG. 3.19 Restaurant flower vases

vases washed when necessary, care being taken that the water is not allowed to become rancid.

If glass vases become green inside they should be scrubbed out using a bottle brush and some salt, after which they should be rinsed, dried and refilled.

Larger flower displays in restaurants may normally be maintained either by the housekeeping department or under contract, but between calls, they may need watering and inspecting for litter (cigarette ends etc), which should be removed.

3.2   TASKS DURING SERVICE

3.2.1   CUSTOMER-BASED ACTIVITIES

3.2.1.1   Welcoming diners

It is an indisputable fact that diners should be made to feel welcome. What a waiter or any member of the food service staff needs to know is what to do and how, in order to achieve the correct result.

In most establishments, it is the duty of one person, usually the Head Waiter, Reception Head Waiter or Hostess to receive, greet and welcome diners on arrival. However, this feeling of 'being welcome' once created on their arrival must linger on throughout their stay in the restaurant. Thus each member of staff plays his own part in creating and maintaining this feeling.

General.
1. On arrival, hold the door open, step aside, and allow diners to enter.
2. Establish a brief eye-contact, smile and pass the time of day.
3. Offer to take coats, wraps, etc.

At this stage it maybe convenient to divide the diners into three broad categories, because each category will need a slightly different approach.

Specific.
1. Newcomers (first visit): A brief and casual mention of perhaps the weather to make contact followed by a statement cum question 'A table for. . . .(four, six, etc)?' – more as a confirmation of the number of persons that you have counted in the party, and that there are no more people joining later.

   Care must be taken to pick up any hesitation on the diner's part regarding the possibility of there having been a reservation made on their behalf by one of their number not yet present, and taken up in a friendly manner. This is a much better approach than to greet erstwhile diners with the question 'Have you booked?' – even with a smile!
2. Infrequent visitors: 'It's nice to see you again. sir.' – A tone of voice must be used that indicates that you really mean it. Avoid using expressions which really say 'I haven't seen *you* for a long time.'
3. Regulars: Develop a suitable style of greeting suited to the restaurant's level of formality to re-affirm to the diner that you recognise that he is a regular customer, such as Good morning/afternoon/evening etc Mr . . ., your usual table . . .?

If the restaurant has a lounge where apéritifs are served, then escort the diners to the lounge, or else to their table, by walking in front of them, guiding the way, making sure that they are following.

Do not leave until you have either handed them over to the sommelier for apéritifs, or the Station Head Waiter. In either case it is good practice to mention the name of the member of staff who will be looking after them, eg 'Peter will be looking after you. Enjoy your meal' or some similar expression.

3.2.1.2 Addressing diners correctly.
Refer to section 2.1.4 'Language and addressing people'.

3.2.1.3   Seating diners

Seating the diners is the first opportunity that the 'station staff' have to make the diners feel welcome. They must make the most of this opportunity. Each party of diners must be treated with the same enthusiasm. Welcoming must never sound like a 'chore' to the diners.

Notes:
1. Having received the diners from the Head Waiter, the Station Head Waiter should pass the time of day with the diners, while they decide amongst themselves how they are going to be seated.
2. The Station Head Waiter should promptly pull out the chair for the eldest lady in the group, while the other station staff should pull out chairs for any other ladies, or older gentlemen in the party.
3. Pull out the chair clear of the table to allow the diner to stand between the table and the chair.
4. As the diner begins to sit down, push in the chair so that the front of the chair very gently touches the back of the legs of the diner. (This re-assures the diner that the chair is in position.)
5. Repeat the gesture until all members of the party are seated, staff and number of diners permitting.
6. Once all diners are seated, the gesture should be made of taking the serviettes from the table and unfolded onto their laps (again, ladies first). Discretion must be used here as most diners nowadays will take charge of their own serviettes.
7. When all diners are seated comfortably, menus should be presented, and while these are being studied, bread rolls should be served, and if it is house custom, water should be offered.

3.2.1.4   Handling wraps and coats

Most first-class establishments make provision for keeping the overcoats and wraps of its customers. Because of the legal implications, (refer to section 4.5, 'Basic legal aspects') the staff must strictly follow the policy of the establishment. If the coats and wraps are collected by the food service staff they must be kept in a secure place not accessible to customers or any other staff.

On arrival, the Head Waiter or the person responsible for reception will offer to take the coats and wraps. As he is to escort the diners, he passes the coats and wraps to a Commis. Ideally, the cloakroom should be equipped with separate hooks for each of the tables and are thus numbered. Once the diners are seated at their table, the cloaks should be neatly hung on the appropriate hooks.

At the time of departure, the coats and wraps should be offered to the diners, the Head Waiter and the Commis should offer to assist the diners in putting on their coats, etc.

3.2.1.5   *Putting diners at their ease*
See section 2.1.4, 'Language and addressing people'.

3.2.1.6   *Conversing with diners*
Note above applies.

3.2.1.7   *Recognising host and/or principal guests*
One of the social skills that every waiter must develop is that of recognising the host and the principal guest amongst the diners. It can hardly be over-emphasised that the host is paying for the meal primarily to entertain his principal guest. Therefore the degree of satisfaction of the host is directly related to the degree of satisfaction of the principal guest.

In addition to the above, certain decisions, such as selection of wine, though influenced by other members of the party, are made by the host. Thus it is important for a waiter to recognise the host without asking.

The skill is basically acquired through observation. The principal guest is likely to be the focus for 'choices of dish' while the host is likely to be the one placing the orders.

The skill cannot be taught, it must be acquired by the individual through awareness and observation.

3.2.1.8   *Handling menus*
Unless a meal has been pre-ordered in the lounge or cocktail bar, a menu (one for each diner) should be offered soon after the apéritif order has been taken, or soon after the guests have been seated.

Method
1. Collect correct number of clean menus from the sideboard. (They should be checked before each service and also before each use). Carry the stack of menus on the right forearm.
2. Approach the diners from the left, left foot forward, and using the left hand, place the menu in front of each diner the right way up (and open – if 'book-type'). Should the diner make to take the menu, lower it gently into his hands, as shown in Fig. 3.20.
3. Return to the sideboard. Allow sufficient time for the diners to make up their minds. Be available to offer assistance if required.
4. Before approaching the table to take the order, collect the order

pad, placing it on a folded service cloth, (on a service plate, if preferred) and enter on it details such as table number, number of covers, date and your signature.

5. Where it is obvious that there is a host, approach the host from the left, stand facing him and await instructions. Do not lean

FIG. 3.20 Handing menus

either on the table or chair-backs and do not bend from the waist or knees.

6. The order is taken for hors-d'oeuvre, and main course with vegetables and potatoes only, at this stage.
7. If each diner is ordering individually, it will be necessary to move to his left before taking the order.

Note: For certain dishes, such as steaks and chops, it will be necessary to enquire about the diner's preference as to the degree of cooking, eg rare, well done etc.

3.2.1.9 Recording the food order

The kitchen needs the order to be recorded in such a fashion that the number of portions of each item can be read easily, irrespective of who has ordered what items, but the waiter needs to know the latter. There is no easy compromise to the situation other than developing a good memory because it is not good practice to take a separate note of the items for his own use, while making out a Kitchen Order Ticket (KOT) as required by the kitchen.

Much will also depend on the type of service practised in the establishment. For plate service it is, of course, necessary to specify a complete main course, including vegetables, etc, but it is better practice with silver service to have the total amount of each item served together by the kitchen, for portioning by the waiter, at the table.

A triplicate checking system permits of the waiter having his own copy of the order without extra writing.

For proper control of such a system everything that is written on a check is charged, and should any item be unacceptable to the diner, or accidentally dropped during service or returned to the kitchen for any other reason, then it must be credited by the cashier through the issue of another check, duly authorised by the Head Waiter or Manager, as follows:

1. For a return – a 'Retour' check is issued.
2. For a replacement – a 'Retour/En Place' check is issued.
3. For an accident – an 'Accident/En Place' is issued.
4. If there is no price difference for an item, then the check should be marked 'n/c'; if there is, then the difference in price should be shown.
5. Dishes served extra to a fixed-price menu should be marked as 'Supplement' or 'Extra', and the price shown.
6. Only the first check of a meal should have the number of covers on it, all following checks being marked 'Suite'.

See section 2.2.12, 'Identifying waiters' checks, bills and bar checks'.

3.2.1.10   Taking the drink order

Orders for drinks may be considered in three distinct categories – ordering of apéritifs, ordering of wines, and ordering of liqueurs and brandies.

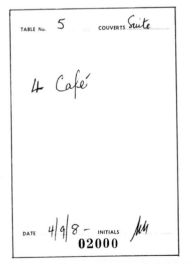
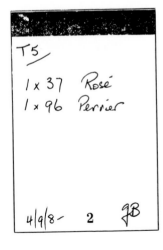

FIG. 3.21 Recording the order: *Top row* (l. to r.): À la carte – Starter and main course; sweet   *Bottom row* (l. to r.) Coffee; Drinks

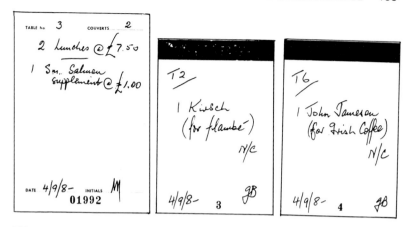

FIG. 3.22 Recording the order: Left Table d'Hôte   Centre & right Accounting
for spirits used in the restaurant

1. Orders for apéritifs will normally be taken either in the foyer, lounge or bar area (outside the restaurant), or at the table. A wine list is not offered, as good-class establishments are expected to provide the majority of apéritifs. It is good salesmanship in taking orders to use a phrase such as 'What may I bring you to drink?', instead of 'Would you like a drink?'. Suggestions for drinks should only be made tactfully.

2. A good wine waiter (Sommelier) would not approach a table to take their order without the knowledge of the food ordered for that table. Therefore it goes without saying that the order for the wines to go with the meal is not normally taken until the food order has been placed, although occasionally the host may place an order for champagne at the time he orders apéritifs. The sommelier should offer the wine list to the host and be ready with spare copies for the other guests, if needed. He should then step back and allow the host time to read and decide on his choice.

   It is good salesmanship to offer a suggestion, using, for example, a phrase such as 'We have a very fine claret, Château . . . . . . , which will go very well with the beef. . . . . However, do not be hasty in offering suggestions; allow sufficient time for the host to read through the wine list and consult with the other diners, especially the principal guest.

3. Orders for liqueurs and brandies should be taken after the sweet course has been cleared but before the coffee is served. Unless requested, a wine list is not presented, nor suggestions offered.

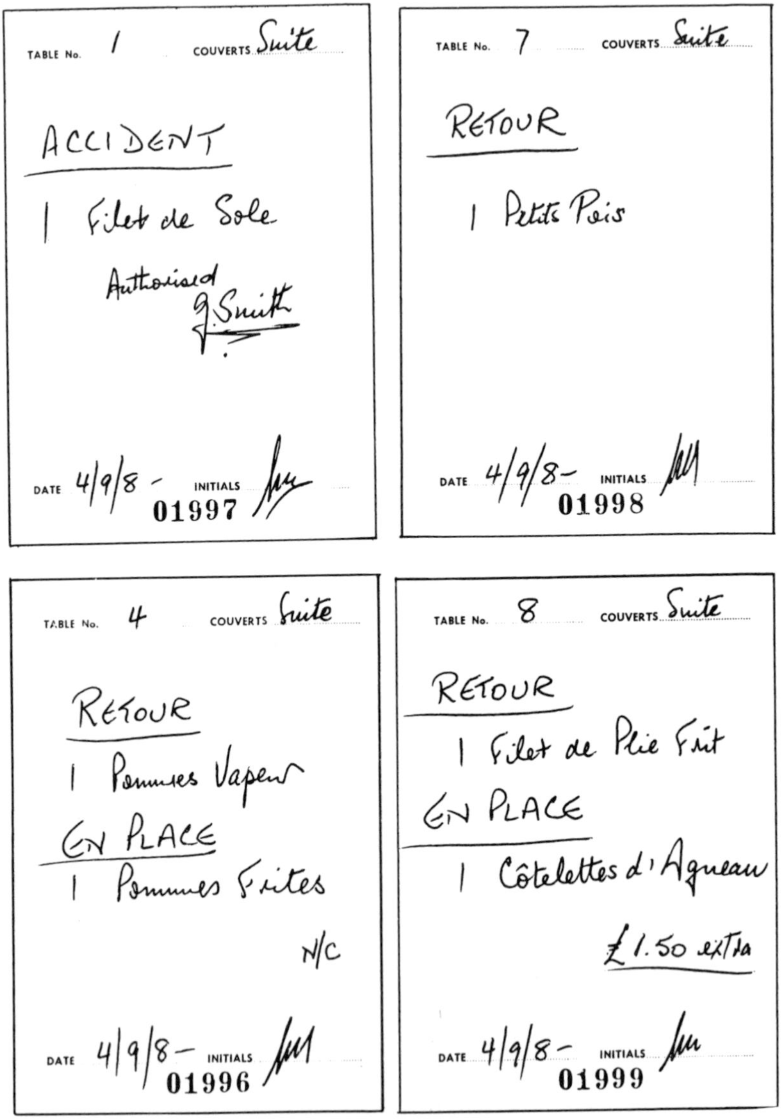

TABLE No. 1	COUVERTS Suite

ACCIDENT

1 Filet de Sole

Authorised
g. Smith

DATE 4/9/8— INITIALS
01997

TABLE No. 7	COUVERTS Suite

RETOUR

1 Petits Pois

DATE 4/9/8— INITIALS
01998

TABLE No. 4	COUVERTS Suite

RETOUR

1 Pommes Vapeur

EN PLACE

1 Pommes Frites

N/C

DATE 4/9/8— INITIALS
01996

TABLE No. 8	COUVERTS Suite

RETOUR

1 Filet de Plie Frit

EN PLACE

1 Côtelettes d'Agneau

£1.50 extra

DATE 4/9/8— INITIALS
01999

FIG. 3.23 Recording the order – Checks for returns etc (see text)

3.2.1.11 *Smoking – procedures regarding lighting etc*

Section 2.3.25 refers to this topic, but waiting staff should always be ready to light diners' cigarettes or cigars when they wish to smoke, and should therefore always carry a gas-filled lighter or matches, for this purpose.

Gas-filled lighters are acceptable for lighting cigars, since there is no smell from the flame; petrol-filled lighters for that reason are not used. Connoisseurs smoking cigars prefer those matches which are not impregnated with paraffin, for the same reason.

Waiters should not offer a light to a diner wishing to smoke a pipe but present a box of matches to the diner so that he may light it himself. (If pipes are permitted in the restaurant.)

3.2.1.12 Dealing with babies, children and handicapped

In many cases food service staff consider babies, children and the handicapped a 'nuisance' because they do not conform to their 'image' of a diner.

There is no justification for this attitude, and all diners should be accorded the same treatment – that of enjoying the 'meal experience'.

The main factor in considering service to babies, children and the handicapped is the need for special seating arrangements which may impede service. Other factors also apply, as follows:

Babies. A well-run restaurant should always have a selection of baby-foods available or be willing to produce them on request. It must also be prepared to heat up milk or any other items that parents may bring with them. Provision should be allowed, where possible for a carry-cot to be placed on two chairs (or a special stand) near to the mother.

Children. Depending on their age may require a high chair or child-seat which can be fixed to an ordinary dining-chair. Consideration should also be made with respect to menus and portion sizes and care should be taken to remove ordinary covers from in front of small children so they do not harm themselves or others at the table with knives, forks, etc.

Handicapped. Wheelchairs, by their very nature, occupy far greater space than a normal dining-chair, therefore they should be positioned in such a way so as to cause least obstruction to the service, while still affording a reasonable view of the restaurant to the diner

For those diners with only one hand or with restricted use, special cutlery is available, but it is common for such customers to bring their own, in which case provision must be made for washing-up these items and returning them at the end of the meal.

TABLE 3.1 Service of a meal

Diners	Station waiter	Commis 1	Commis 2
1. Arrive 2. Seated at table 3. Studying menu	Greets and assists in seating Offers menus Waits attentively by sideboard ready to offer assistance or suggestions	Assists in seating Offers water Waits by sideboard after removing any spare covers.	Assists in seating Collects bread rolls, melba toast, butter etc from still-room and brings them to sideboard
4. Ready to place order 5. Awaiting first course	Takes the order Passes order to Commis 2 and takes duplicate to Cashier	Waits by sideboard Places butter dish on table and serves bread rolls	Takes order to kitchen and waits to collect first course
At this stage the Wine Waiter will take order for any wines to be served with the meal			
6. Awaiting first course	Adjusts cover for each diner	Gets cold plates ready. Collects hors d'oeuvre trolley. Places réchaud plates on sideboard top.	Returns with first course and unloads on sideboard, assisted by Commis 1
7. Eating first course	2. Serves starters on plates – cold first Attends to other diners or tasks	1. Places plates in front of diners	3. Offers any dressings or accompaniments Clears the service dishes to the wash-up. Returns and waits by sideboard.
8. Finished first course	Relieves Commis 1 to assist Commis 2 in collecting main course	Clears first-course plates to sideboard. Replaces réchaud plates Prepares for service of main course – places new réchaud plates on top of sideboard. Goes to kitchen and assists Commis 2 in collecting main course	Assists Commis 1 and clears first-course plates to wash-up Waits and collects main course, assisted by Commis 1
9. Awaiting main course	2. Serves main course	1. Places joint plates in front of diners 4. Serves vegetables	3. Serves potatoes
10. Eating main course	Attends to other diners or tasks	Serves sauces and accompaniments Waits by sideboard – anticipating needs of diners Replaces réchaud dishes	Clears main-course service dishes to kitchen and returns to sideboard

11. Finished main course	Attends to other diners or tasks	Clears main course plates to sideboard "Crumbs-down" and "brings-down" dessert spoon & fork	Clears side plates and knives to sideboard. Clears cruets and water-glasses, if not required. Clears main-course plates to wash-up and returns to sideboard
12. Awaiting sweet course	Takes order for the sweet course (hot or cold)	Presents sweet trolley (if it is to be presented). Serves sweet course on plates	Takes order from Station Waiter for hot sweets and collects. Places served plates in front of diners
13. Eating sweet course		Waits by the sideboard	Waits by the sideboard
14. Finished sweet course		Clears sweet-course plates to sideboard	Clears sweet-course plates to wash-up
15. Awaiting coffee	Takes order for liqueurs (if not done by Wine Waiter)	Prepares plates, saucers and spoons for coffee service. Serves coffee	Collects coffee cups, coffee and milk
16. During coffee		Places ashtray on table, if required	
17. Request bill	Collects bill from Cashier. Returns bill and settlement to Cashier. Returns change and receipt to diner.	Waits by sideboard	Waits by sideboard
18. Ready to leave	Wishes 'good-bye' and moves chairs out	Assists station waiter – helps with coats and wraps etc.	Fetches coats, wraps, etc. Helps station waiter
19. Departed	Checks for any diners' property	Re-lays table	Assists Commis 1

3.2.2 WAITER-BASED ACTIVITIES

3.2.2.1 Service of a meal

Table 3.1 shows the chronological service of a typical meal in a first-class restaurant employing a full chef and commis system.

It is, of necessity, only a synopsis, and can in no way be taken as definitive and will depend on both levels of staff employed and house custom.

3.2.2.2 Offering bread rolls

In most establishments bread rolls and butter are offered as part of the cover, and included in the 'cover charge', if any. The service of bread rolls should be carried out while the diners are 'studying' the menu (before taking the food order).

Method
1. Collect fresh butter from the Still Room. Place the butter dish on a doily, on a side-plate. Add a butter-knife and place near to the centre of the table.

Note: Tables of more than four covers will require more than one butter dish, placed along the centre line of the table, so that four diners can share one.
2. Place the bread roll basket on a folded service cloth on the open palm of the left hand with a service spoon and fork in the right.
3. Approach each diner from the left, left foot forward, and serve the bread roll onto the side-plate.

3.2.2.3 Serving water

The timing for serving water differs from one establishment to another. In some establishments water is served in the 'American style' as soon as the diners are seated at the table. In the opinion of the authors it is preferable to delay the service of water until the wine order, if any, has been taken. This procedure avoids the unnecessary clutter of 'water-glasses' on the table.

Method
1. Collect iced-water jug from the sideboard on a serviette-covered dessert-plate, on a folded service cloth on the palm of the left hand.
2. Approach the diner from the right, foot forward.
3. Keeping the jug behind the diner's back and using the right

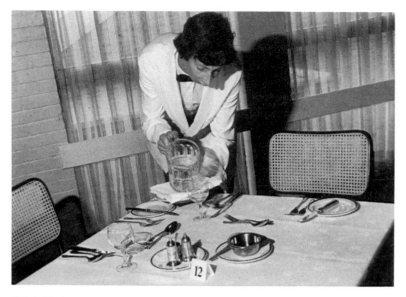

FIG. 3.24 Serving of water

hand, turn up the glass (if not already turned up by the somme-lier or before the service).
4. Make sure that the diner is aware that you are about to serve water. Move the left hand so that the water jug is near the glass.
5. Serve water by tilting the water jug, so that the base still rests on the serviette on the plate; as shown in Figure 3.24.

Note: It is best to use a linen serviette under the water jug rather than a doily because condensation will make the doily wet and fall to pieces.

3.2.2.4 *Changing cover prior to serving first course*
It is important that each diner has only the correct cutlery for his entire meal. The cover should therefore be adjusted, if necessary, after the order has been taken and definitely BEFORE serving the first course. The best person to carry out this task is the one who takes the order (usually the Station Head Waiter or Station Waiter).

Method
1. Refer to the order and identify the extra cutlery required for each diner.
2. Collect the extra cutlery on a Service Plate or Service Salver lined with a serviette.

3. For adjusting forks approach from the left, and for adjusting knives or soup spoons approach from the right of the diner. Never reach across.

4. Using first finger and thumb, remove first any surplus cutlery by lifting from the middle of the stem and place it on the Service Salver. Replace or add any additional cutlery required before moving onto the other side of the diner.

5. Repeat with each diner, until all covers have been adjusted.

3.2.2.5   Identifying the following menu items and their accompaniments with the necessary equipment for their service

It is necessary for the waiter to be prepared to advise diners on their choice of dishes, therefore it is important for waiting staff to know at least the content of the menu in the establishment in which they work, but preferably, and with experience, acquire a wider knowledge of menu content.

This subject is covered more fully in Chapter 4 sections 4.1 and 4.2, and here we cover only the service of both standard and non-standard items to be found on the menu, under general heading.

Hors-d'oeuvre

As a menu heading, this item covers hors-d'oeuvre proper, both hot and cold, as well as hors-d'oeuvre substitutes.

Fruit juices. (Jus des Fruits)   These are served in a small-stemmed goblet (5 oz) or similar on a side-plate with doily and teaspoon. Pass caster sugar in dredger.

Tomato Juice. (Jus de Tomate)   These are served in a small-stemmed goblet (5 oz) or similar on side-plate with doily and teaspoon. Pass bottle of shaken Worcester Sauce (capless) on a doily-covered side-plate. Ensure salt and pepper (mill) are on table.

Fruit Cocktails. (Cocktails des Fruits . . . Florida, etc)   These are usually served from the kitchen in Paris goblets or glass or metal coupes. Present on doily-covered side-plate with teaspoon. Pass sugar dredger. Melon cocktail might be served in the melon shell if Charentais or Ogen.

Half-Grapefruit. (Demi-Pamplemousse)   These may be prepared in either kitchen or restaurant, using a sharp knife. All segments to be cut away separately from membranes, starting radially from centre, first removing core; then cutting the outside edges. Each segment to be loose. Garnish with glacé or cocktail cherry and a teaspoon of caster sugar. Serve in a coupe on a doily-covered side-plate with a grapefruit spoon or teaspoon. Pass sugar dredger.

Melon. (Melon)   The service of melon will depend on the actual melon to be served. Some are served in slices (Honeydew, Elche), others whole (Charentais, Ogen, Rock, Canteloupe). In most establishments, melon will be prepared in the kitchen.

Melons served whole (usually with top and seeds removed) may be served in coupes or small glass or china bowls, placed on a doily-covered side-plate. The cover is a dessert-spoon.

Sliced melon segments should be served direct onto a sideplate. The cover should be a dessert-spoon and fork, unless parma ham is served with the melon, in which case a dessert-knife may replace the dessert-spoon.

A service of caster-sugar and powdered ginger should be passed together with a sugar dredger. Alternatively, a mixture of 1 part ginger to 10 parts sugar may be kept for service of melon.

Avocado pear. (Avocat)   A portion consists of half of an avocado pear cut lengthwise with the stone removed. This may be served on a side-plate on a bed of lettuce, or in a special avocado-shaped dish, or a coupe. Garnish will depend on menu name and will normally be served dressed from kitchen. The dish is presented at table on doily-covered side-plate. The cover is a teaspoon, with oyster fork, if filled with seafood. Finger-bowl and serviette is also served.

Mixed Hors-d'Oeuvre. (Hors-d'Oeuvre Varié)   Denotes a selection of small tasty items composed of meat, fish, vegetables, or a combination, often in a sauce, or vinegar/oil dressing. Usually highly seasoned and intended to stimulate the palate for the other dishes to follow in the meal.

Hors-d'oeuvre will normally be served in one of three ways, depending on the custom of the house, and whether offered as part of a table d'hôte menu, or an à la carte menu. These are as follows:-
Plated – on a side-plate for table d'hôte, or a fish-plate for à la carte, dressed in the kitchen.
Tray – A sectioned hors-d'oeuvre tray containing a selection of about six items will be presented to each diner in turn, who will be served a small quantity form each section, onto a fish-plate, using spoon and fork.

Note: Separate service cutlery for each item.

Trolley – Usually a drum-shaped rotating trolley fitted with some 12 to 18 different items, according to size, will be wheeled to the table and the diner allowed to make a selection, being given a clear view of what is available. The waiter will stand behind the trolley serving the items onto a fish-plate held in either his left hand, or on a plate rest, if fitted to the trolley. After serving one diner, the waiter moves the trolley to the next before serving him.

An oil and vinegar cruet is always placed on the table when hors-d'oeuvre are served, and both pepper mill and cayenne pepper will be offered, depending on the content of the selection.

The list of possible items for inclusion in an hors-d'oeuvre varié is endless and depends to a great extent on the imagination of the chef, but some of the more common items are given below:

Fish	**Meat**	**Vegetables**
Sardines in oil	Salami cornets	Russian salad
Sardines in tomato	Garlic sausage	Beetroot in vinegar
Tuna fish	Ox-cheek salad	Pickled gherkins
Smoked herring fillet	Ham cornets	Mushrooms à la Grecque
Rollmop herrings	Italian salad	Tomato salad
Smoked eel	Chicken salad	Cauliflower florets
Smoked salmon cornets	Egg mayonnaise	Sliced cucumber
Smoked sprats		Potato salad
Fish mayonnaise		
Bismarck herring		
Soused herring		
Anchovy fillets		

The cover for hors-d'oeuvre was traditionally a fish cover, but now all knife blades are made of stainless steel, a dessert knife and fork is acceptable, especially if there is a meat content in the hors-d'oeuvre.

Oysters (Huitres)   Now normally to be found only in high-class or speciality restaurants, due to their high cost, oysters are still popular. The portion is usually reckoned in half-dozens.

Oysters are served from the kitchen, opened, in the deep shell, on a bed of ice, in either special oyster-plates, with seven indentations (6 for the oysters, and the centre one for a half-lemon) or a soup-plate on an under-plate.

The cover for oysters is an oyster-fork placed at 45° on the right of the joint-knife, and a finger-bowl containing tepid water with a slice of lemon, and a napkin.

Adjuncts for the service of oysters are thinly-cut buttered brown bread, Tabasco sauce, chilli vinegar, tarragon vinegar, mignonnette pepper, or a pepper-mill, cayenne pepper, and some diners, especially if European, will want tomato ketchup.

Note: In restaurants with a large oyster trade, the above (apart from the brown bread) are usually known as the 'oyster cruet', and may well be contained in a metal container with fitting glass containers.

Caviar (Caviare)   Rarely found in most restaurants due to its high cost, caviar comes in several types, the best quality being known as Beluga. It is sold in tins with removeable lids, and once opened must be kept refrigerated. It is served from the kitchen in its tin, placed on a silver dish, and surrounded by crushed ice. The tin is weighed before serving, and afterwards, the diner being charged for the amount consumed, by weight, although the normal portion of one dessertspoon or two teaspoonsful is approximately one ounce (30 grams).

Caviar should be spooned from the tin using a horn, bone or glass spoon.

The cover is a cold fish plate and caviar knife on the right-hand side of the cover. Should a caviar knife not be available, then a fish knife will serve.

Adjuncts to the service of caviar are brown bread, hot breakfast toast or blinis (buckwheat pancakes), butter, halves of lemon wrapped in muslin, finely chopped shallots, sieved hard-boiled eggs (yolk and white separately), and chopped parsley, together with pepper-mill and cayenne pepper.

Finger-bowls with tepid water and slice of lemon, and a napkin, are also placed for each diner.

Pâté de Foie Gras   A speciality of Strasbourg, this pâté of fattened goose livers comes either in a stone-ware lidded container (*terrine*) or in a tunnel-shaped tin (*bloc tunnel*). If in a terrine, it will be presented on a silver dish in a bed of crushed ice. A portion (one dessertspoonful) will be served onto a cold fish plate using a dessert-spoon previously heated by plunging into a jug of hot water. (N.B. Do not use boiling water in a glass jug unless it will withstand the heat, e.g. 'Pyrex', 'Duralex' or similar.)

The tunnel-shaped foie gras will usually be served from the kitchen in slices on a bed of lettuce.

The cover is a dessert-knife and a cold fish plate.

Adjuncts are crustless hot toast and butter.

Pâté (du Chef, Maison, en Croûte etc.) A potted meat either in a round or loaf-shaped stone-ware dish, or pastry-case, usually containing liver and other meats according to name etc.

Portion will be one slice (about 1/2″ thick (1 cm)).

Cover as above.

Adjuncts as above, but if in a pastry-case or on a bed of lettuce, then a dessert fork should be included.

Gull's Eggs/Plover's Eggs (Oeufs de Mouette/Oeufs de Pluvier)   Will often appear on menus priced individually and served hard-boiled (cold). The portion is usually three eggs.

Cover is a fish plate and dessert knife and fork, with a sideplate for the shells. A fingerbowl containing tepid water and lemon and a spare napkin is also served.

Adjuncts are cut brown bread and butter and Oriental salt (a mixture of salt, celery seed and cayenne pepper).

Potted Shrimps   A speciality from Morecambe Bay, these small shelled shrimps are cooked, spiced and set in clarified butter. Usually sold in cartons, one carton constituting a portion, which will be sent from the kitchen on a bed of shredded lettuce together with a quarter of lemon.

Cover is a fish knife and fork and a cold fish plate.

Adjuncts are cut brown bread and butter and cayenne pepper.

Smoked Salmon (Saumon Fumé)   Cut paper-thin from a side of smoked salmon as near parallel to the skin as possible. This may be cut in the kitchen, in which case it will be presented in overlapping slices on a silver flat, or plated; or if carved from a board in the restaurant, either on a buffet or trolley in front of the diner, it will be plated. The garnish will be 1/4 or 1/2 lemon.

The cover will be a fish plate and fish knife and fork.

Service will be carried out using a joint fork, rolling the slice onto the fork by introducing the end of the first slice between two prongs. The slice will then be unrolled onto the pate.

Adjuncts for service are thin-cut brown bread and butter, and cayenne pepper.

Note: If kept in the restaurant during the service, the top surface of the smoked-salmon should be rubbed lightly with oil prior to the service, to enhance its appearance.

Shrimp or Prawn Cocktail (Cocktail des Crevettes Grises ou Crev-

ettes Roses)   Shrimp or prawn cocktail consists of peeled shrimps or prawns on a bed of shredded lettuce, coated with sauce Marie-Rose, either in a Paris goblet, or a silver-plated seafood-cocktail cup (a double, footed cup allowing crushed ice to be placed in the outside container).

Service of either vessel to be on a sideplate with a paper doily.

Cover is a teaspoon and seafood fork, placed points towards each other, on the sideplate of the cocktail, with the spoon on the right-hand side.

Adjuncts are 1/4 lemon, thin-cut brown bread and butter, and cayenne pepper.

Note: Should the cocktail be garnished with a whole prawn placed over the side of the glass or cup, a finger-bowl containing tepid water with a slice of lemon, and a spare napkin must also be served.

Prawns or Shrimps (Crevettes Roses ou Crevettes Grises)   Prawns of any size, or shrimps, often form a dish serving as an hors-d'oeuvre substitute.

After boiling, they may be served hot, cold or fried. Served unpeeled, they may be sent from the kitchen on a dish of crushed ice or round the rim of a Paris goblet (*en Promenade*) if cold.

If hot, they will be served on a silver flat garnished with 1/4 lemon.

Cover is a cold or hot fish plate depending on the dish character, with a soup-plate for debris and a finger-bowl with tepid water and a slice of lemon, together with a spare napkin.

Adjuncts are 1/4 lemon and thin-cut brown bread and butter.

Smoked Trout (Truite Fumée)   This will usually be served whole from the kitchen and must be presented to the diner before removing to the sideboard or guéridon, where it should have head and skin removed, the two fillets then being separated and placed on a cold fish plate, together with any garnish sent from the kitchen, skin-side uppermost.

The cover will be a fish knife and fork.

Adjuncts are 1/4 lemon, thin-cut brown bread and butter, cayenne pepper, and a pepper-mill. Horse-radish sauce should be passed.

Smoked Mackerel (Maquereau Fumé)   As Smoked Trout above.

Smoked Eel (Anguille Fumée)   As Smoked Trout, but without the horse radish sauce.

Snails (Escargots)   Snails, specially prepared with garlic-butter and sold in either portions of 6, 9, or 12.

They are presented either in their shells or porcelain shells in the indentations of a snail dish, with the opening upwards so that the hot garlic butter does not run out.

The service is a snail dish on a hot fish plate with a doily.

The cover is a snail fork and teaspoon on the right of the cover, and snail tongs on the left.

Adjuncts are thin-cut brown bread and butter, or hot breakfast toast.

Basic soups (Potages)

For full description of types of soups, see section 4.1.3.

In high-class restaurants, all soups except four are served in the same manner.

The standard cover is a hot soup-plate, with a joint or fish-plate as 'liner' or under-plate, and a soup spoon on the diner's right-hand side. It is arguable whether a hot or cold plate should be used as a liner, but a liner is essential for first-class service.

Service will depend on whether one portion or more of the same soup is to be served to the table.

If one portion only is to be served, a single-portion tureen will be brought from the kitchen, the soup-plate and liner will be put down in front of the diner from the left, while also carrying the tureen on a service-plate or small salver.

The soup is then poured into the soup-plate, pouring away from the diner, using the right hand, while protecting the diner's lap from drips etc, with the service-plate in the left hand.

For service of more than one portion of the same soup see section 2.3.10, 'Serving using a ladle from a tureen'.

Adjuncts and accompaniments will depend on the soup in question and waiting staff should be aware of these in case the kitchen do not present them at the time of service. See list at end of this section.

The four types of soup requiring special note are as follows:

Consommés (Hot or cold).   Consommés are served in consommé cups (a two-handled cup) on a saucer placed on a sweet or fish plate with a doily.

Note: The cover for consommé is traditionally a dessert spoon, *not* a soup spoon. Cups should be hot for hot consommé and cold for cold or jellied consommés.

Petite marmite.   This is served in a small, lidded earthenware pot (one per portion) placed on a sweet plate with a doily. Served to diner, with lid removed, from left.

The cover is dessert spoon (and fork, should the soup contain chicken winglets).

Turtle Soup (Tortue Claire).   Usually served in cups, as consommé, but may be served in soup-plates. At one time turtle soup was served in special cups slightly larger than a coffee 'demie-tasse', but these are now extremely rare.

Adjuncts for the service of soups

Croûte au Pot	Toasted, diagonal-cut slice of small French loaf (flûte) and grated parmesan cheese.
Soupe à l'oignon	As above.
Petite marmite	As above.
Minestrone	Grated parmesan cheese.
Potage St Germain	Croûtons (fried, diced white bread (half-cm cubes).
Bouillabaisse	Toasted french-bread slices.
Tortue Claire	Sherry (heated in ladle before adding to soup), thin cut brown bread and butter, quarter-lemon, and cheese straws (passed).
Bortsch à la Russe	Sour cream, beetroot juice, piroshkis (Tiny duck-filled patties).

Farinaceous dishes (Farineux)

Mainly of Italian origin, they include all pasta items, savoury rice dishes and gnocchi.

The majority will be served on silver flats, often with the sauce separately (*à part*), but some sauced items may be served from the kitchen in single, eared fireproof dishes. If presented on silver then they will be served to the diner on a hot fish-plate, unless for a main course item. If on a fireproof dish this will be served on a fish-plate with a doily.

The cover will vary according to the dish. For spaghetti, a joint fork on the right-hand side, with a dessert spoon on the left. For all other items, a dessert spoon and fork, with the fork on the left.

Adjunct for all pasta dishes is grated parmesan cheese, sprinkled over the top of the pasta. Once served, using a dessert spoon, the cheese is then removed. It is not left on the table.

Egg dishes (oeufs)
Eggs will be found on lunch and dinner menus in all forms except boiled, which will only appear on breakfast menus. The methods normally found will be poached (*poché*), coddled (*mollet*), fried (*sur le plat*), scrambled (*brouillés*), 'en cocotte', or as omelets (*omelettes*).

Egg dishes will normally be served onto hot fish-plates except an omelet served as a main course, when a joint-plate will be used. Eggs 'en cocotte' will be served on a side-plate with a doily if 1 is served, or on a fish-plate with doily if two are served as a portion.

The cover used is a joint fork (on right-hand side) for omelets if served alone, otherwise a joint knife and fork. For other egg dishes, a dessert knife and fork, except for the following:

Oeufs en cocotte	Teaspoon
Oeufs sur le plat	Desert spoon and fork
Omelette Arnold Bennett	Fish knife and fork

Note:
1. Cold egg dishes will normally appear on menus as hors-d'oeuvre.
2. Ends of omelets will normally require removal before service if well cooked. Some diners prefer omelets to be slightly runny (*baveuse*) in the centre, and should be asked when taking their order.

Fish dishes (Poissons)
The many different kinds of fresh and salt-water fish lend themselves to different methods of cookery, such as poaching, grilling, deep or shallow-frying and boiling (see also section 4.1.3).

The size of the fish and method of cooking will determine the way in which it is served.

Poached fish (Poché).   Small fish. Usually cooked in fillets, either flat, folded or rolled, and usually served coated with a sauce. A portion would normally be one or two fillets with garnish, if any. Small round fish such as trout etc, may also be poached, in which case they are served whole.

Large fish. Prime fish such as salmon (*saumon*) or turbot (*turbot*) are often cooked whole and served whole, especially for banqueting, buffets, etc., but they can also be cut into steaks or cutlets (*darnes*). Other large fish, such as cod (*cabillaud*) or haddock (*aigrefin*) may be served in the same way. Before service, the skin must be removed from these steaks by rolling it off onto the prongs of a fork from the back to the belly, one side at a time, and the centre bone removed.

Debris must be put onto another plate and the fish is served from the silver flat.

Shallow-fried fish (à la meuniere, Belle-Meunière, etc). Usually used for fish served whole, such as trout, sole, etc. The dish is presented to the diner who should be asked whether he wishes the head removed, or the fish filleted (in the case of sole). Should he so require, the dish is taken to the sideboard or guéridon where the operation will be carried out. Debris is removed to another plate and the fish served.

Deep-fried fish (Frit(e)). For deep-fried soles the above notes regarding service are also valid.

Deep-fried fillets and whitebait are served in the normal way.

Grilled fish (Grillé(e)). For soles etc, and fillets, see under Shallow-fried. For cod steaks etc, see under Poached Fish.

Boiled fish (Bouilli). Mainly used in invalid cookery, but cod steaks sometimes appear on lunch menus. Treat as poached.

Note: Fish is served on a fish-plate other than for a main course, when it will be served on a joint-plate, hot for hot fish, cold for cold fish. The cover is fish knife and fork.

Adjuncts for the service of fish depend on the dish in question. Those dishes consisting of poached fillets or steaks of fish with a sauce will require nothing else. The sauce will depend on the name of the dish. The various adjuncts are listed below.

Poached fish. A rich sauce based on eggs and/or butter such as Hollandaise, Butter sauce, Egg sauce or melted butter.

Poached salmon – Hot. Hollandaise sauce, or Sauce Mousseline, cucumber salad, new potatoes.

Poached Salmon – Cold. Mayonnaise, cucumber salad.

Grilled Fish. A compound butter, such as Anchovy butter, or Maître d'Hôtel, melted butter, Butter sauce, Hollandaise or Mousseline.

Deep-fried fish (in batter) (Poisson Frit à l'Orly). Tomato sauce. (*egged and breadcrumbed*) (*Poisson Frit à l'Anglaise*). Quarter-lemon, fried parsley, and sauce tartare.

Shell-fish (Les Crustacés). Prawns, shrimps and oysters are dealt with under Hors-d'Oeuvre. For the fish course, the main shell-fish to be considered is the lobster (*Homard*) and to a lesser extent the crawfish (*Langouste*). Both may be served hot or cold, in the shell or out, but for the purpose of the present volume we will consider the portion and presentation to be half a lobster which will be prepared and dished in the larder or kitchen.

Service will be on a joint-plate with a spare one for debris. The cover is a fish cover together with a lobster pick, and if the diner wishes to remove the flesh from the claws himself, a pair of lobster crackers. A finger bowl containing tepid water with a slice of lemon, with a napkin is also placed near to hand.

Adjuncts for service are mayonnaise with the garnish from the kitchen, if cold, or sauce as detailed on the menu if hot.

Note:
1. Crawfish are treated identically except that no crackers are required in the cover.
2. Mussels (*Moules à la Marinière*) are served into a soup-plate with underplate, and a dessert spoon is placed together with the fish cover. Brown bread and butter and pepper-mill is also served.
3. Shrimps and prawns may be served hot sauced, curried, or Provençale, etc., in which case they are shelled and served as a normal fish dish.

Meat dishes (Viandes)
The rules of service for all meat dishes are simple. With the exception of entrées served as a separate course (which call for an entrée plate (8 in), curries or Irish stew (which both call for a soup-plate,) all meat dishes are served from silver flats or dishes on to joint-plates (usually 10 in) or oval platters.

The cover is a joint knife and fork, with a dessert spoon added for Irish stew, and a dessert spoon and fork for curries. For steaks, knives with serrated edges are laid, and if the standard joint knife has a plain edge, then some restaurants will have some special steak knives for this purpose.

Service is carried out with service spoon and fork, serving the meat at the bottom of the plate (nearest to the diner) for all meat dishes except curries, when the rice pilaw will be served in a ring on the plate first, with the curry placed in the centre.

The actual dish concerned will determine the proper adjuncts to be used. These are as follows:

Roast meats.

Beef   – Roast gravy. Yorkshire pudding, Horseradish sauce.
Pork   – Roast gravy. Sage & Onion stuffing, Apple sauce.
Veal   – Roast gravy. Parsley, thyme & lemon stuffing.
Lamb   – Roast gravy. Mint sauce or Mint jelly.
Mutton – Roast gravy. Red current jelly or Onion sauce.

Braised meats.

Ham   – Madeira sauce, spinach (leaf or purée).
Beef   – According to menu name.
Tongue – As ham.

Grilled meats.

Steaks   – Watercress, a compound butter such as Maître
                 d'Hôtel, or Sauce Béarnaise (for Châteaubriands),
                 French or English mustard to be passed, or
                 sauced as per menu name.
Ham, Gammon   – as per menu name.

Other meat dishes.

Curries   – Pilaw rice (see above), Bombay Duck,
                     poppadums, chutney, and often a selection
                     of sliced or diced fruits etc (banana,
                     cucumber, apple, sultanas) and coconut.
Lancashire Hot-Pot – Pickled red cabbage.
Irish stew   – Worcestershire sauce.
Cold meat   – Pickles, chutneys, mustards.
Sausages   – English or French mustard.

Poultry and Game (Volaille et Gibier)
Cover and service as for meat dishes (above).
    Adjuncts for the various dishes are as follows:

Roast poultry.

Chicken — Roast gravy, watercress, bread sauce, game chips, streaky bacon rasher or bacon roll.

Duck — Roast gravy, apple sauce, sage and onion stuffing.

Goose — As Duck.

Turkey — Roast gravy, chipolata sausage, bacon roll, sage and onion or chestnut stuffing, or braised chestnuts, cranberry sauce.

Roast game birds.

Pheasant — Roast gravy, game chips, bread sauce, fried white breadcrumbs, all served in sauce-boats.

Grouse — As pheasant.

Partridge — As pheasant.

Other game dishes.

Stews (*Salmis*) — Red currant jelly.

Jugged hare — As stews.

Hare (roast) — As stews, also with chestnut purée, forcemeat balls.

Venison — Red currant jelly, Cumberland sauce.

Vegetables (Légumes)

While in the classic French style, prime vegetables are usually served as a separate course (*entremet de légumes*), or as an hors-d'oeuvre substitute, others are only served as a garnish to meat or other dishes. Potatoes are also mainly served as a garnish. In Britain, vegetables are invariably served as an accompaniment to a main course, other than those served as an hors-d'oeuvre substitute.

The prime vegetables include asparagus, globe artichokes, corn-on-the-cob, and broccoli, and will usually be served with a sauce, as follows:

Asparagus, hot — Melted butter or Hollandaise sauce.

Asparagus, cold — Vinaigrette sauce or mayonnaise.

Globe artichokes, hot — As asparagus.

Globe artichokes, cold — As asparagus.

Corn-on-the-cob, hot — Melted butter.

Broccoli, hot — Hollandaise sauce.

Cauliflower may be served as either a garnish or a dish in its own right, such as Cauliflower Mornay. Nowadays, jacket potatoes have become popular as a snack dish with various fillings, or as a side-dish to a main course. Each potato is cut on top in the form of a cross which is then pinched together to open it, and a pat of butter, cream cheese and chives or other filling is placed inside. They would be served on a side-plate.

Note: Prime vegetables will normally be served onto entrée-plates, except asparagus, which will be served onto a joint-plate, and the plates for hot asparagus and globe artichokes will be tilted away from the diner by placing a joint fork upside-down under the edge nearest to the diner in order to direct the melted butter into one place, so that the vegetable may be dipped into it.

Globe artichokes are eaten with the fingers, as asparagus may be, if asparagus tongs are not available; therefore a finger-bowl with tepid water and slice of lemon with a napkin are served.

Asparagus may be presented from the kitchen in two ways; on a serviette-covered flat, or in an asparagus-dish with a perforated drainer.

Salads (Salades)

Salads found in the classic restaurant situation can be one of two sorts, a compound salad (*salade composée*) prepared in the kitchen, such as Salade Niçoise or Salade Waldorf; or a plain salad such as a green salad (*salade verte*), or a mixed salad (*salade panachée*). These are prepared in the kitchen, but dressed at the table in the restaurant, using one of the standard dressings (see below).

The salad, after dressing, will be served usually onto a salad crescent which will be placed at the left upper part of the joint plate, and will have a dessert fork placed on it, prongs downwards, the handle pointing towards the side-plate ie about 30 degrees from the centre line of the cover to which it relates.

Should salad crescents not be available, wooden or glass salad bowls of a suitable size (about 6 in maximum) are acceptable for single portions.

In order to dress salads, the following should be assembled:

Soup Plate	joint fork	salt	pepper mill
Oil	vinegar	caster sugar	English mustard
French mustard			

Note: Oil used should be either olive, corn or ground-nut, and the best vinegar is a wine vinegar, preferably white.

The diner should be asked whether he wishes you to dress the salad. If so, a mixture of salt, pepper, mustard and sugar (if desired) is moistened with vinegar and mixed together in the soup-plate with the fork. Oil is then added and the consistency corrected with more vinegar or oil if necessary to give a proportion of 1 part vinegar to 3 parts of oil, or according to the diner's requirements.

The dressing is then spooned over the salad which is then turned in the dressing to coat all surfaces using a spoon and fork before arranging neatly on the salad crescent.

Lettuce should be torn into small pieces with the spoon and fork before dressing and should not be cut with a knife to prevent 'bleeding'.

The dressing given above is a simple 'vinaigrette' or 'French' dressing and is the basis for many others.

Full details of these can be found in *"Modern Restaurant Service"*, J Fuller (Hutchinson) 1983.

Sorbets

These are fruit or liqueur-flavoured water-ices, traditionally served during a banquet between relevé and roast, with Russian cigarettes as a break during the meal and to aid digestion. They are usually serted in a small, tall glass served on a side plate with doily.

Sweets (Entremets)

Sweets require no special notes, because they are invariably served from the kitchen/pastry section either on silver flats or in coupes. If on silver, the normal rules of service apply, with sauces being served after the sweet, onto a $7\frac{1}{2}$ in or 8 in plate; if served in coupes, then the coupe will be placed on a doily on a side plate, with a teaspoon.

Wafers, biscuits, etc, will normally be served separately on a doileyed side plate, or passed by the waiter to each diner in turn.

Note: Before serving the sweet course, the table is cleared of all items except water or wine-glasses in use, including cruets, and then crumbed-down, bringing the spoon and fork, if laid, down in front of the diner.

The normal cover for sweets is a dessert spoon and fork, except as stated above for coupes, and if fresh fruit is to be served, see below.

Should a savoury be required instead of a sweet, see below.

Savouries (Savoureux)

Served in the same manner as meat dishes with a spoon and fork onto hot sweet-or entrée-plates.

Cover is dessert knife and fork, even if savoury contains fish.

Adjuncts will depend on the content of the savoury, but salt and pepper, cayenne pepper, pepper-mill and Worcestershire sauce, together with tomato ketchup, a fruit sauce, and English and French mustard should be available and offered to diners.

Cheeses (Fromages)

Cheeses can be served in the Continental fashion (ie before the sweet course), or in the English fashion (after the sweet course.)

If a selection of cheeses is on the menu then they will be either presented to the diner on a cheese board or from a cheese trolley, and served to him by the waiter, onto a side-plate.

The cover is a dessert knife (and fork, in the best-class establishments), or dessert spoon and fork for Petite Suisse, which is always served with caster sugar.

Adjuncts are butter pats and mixed cheese biscuits, (including digestive), bread rolls or French bread (with oat-cakes for the Scottish Crowdie cheese).

Sticks of celery and radishes are usually served, and spring onions, mixed pickles, mustard and apples may be required by diners, and should always be available.

Note: Separate knives and forks should always be used for each type of cheese on a cheese board

For methods of cutting different types of cheeses, see section 4.2.4.

Fresh fruit (Fruits Frais)

Fresh fruit, other than that served as an hors-d'oeuvre substitute (eg melon, grapefruit, etc) or pineapple which is usually prepared either in the kitchen, or using guéridon service, will be presented by the waiter to the diner, contained in a fruit basket for the diner to help himself.

Cover is a side plate, with fruit knife and fork presented on the side plate with the knife point placed between the prongs of the fork, and spread to a wide angle, together with a finger-bowl containing tepid water with a slice of lemon, placed on a doily-covered side plate, together with a napkin.

The waiter will bring the fruit basket to the table together with a bowl of cold water in which to rinse grapes or cherries, if served.

Should grapes be presented in large bunches, a pair of grape scissors should be at hand, and a suitably-sized bunch cut and dipped into the water, the waiter having placed the bowl conveniently on

TABLE 3.2   Sauces used in the restaurant

	Roux-based sauces						Butter-based sauces	Oil-based sauces	
Roux	Blond	Blanc	Blanc	Blanc	Blanc	Blanc			
Liquid/stock	Brown Stock	Veal Stock	Veal Stock	Fish Stock	Chicken Stock	Milk			
Basic sauce	Espagnole (Brown Sauce)	Fond de Veau Lié (Thickened Veal Stock)	Sauce Tomate (Tomato Sauce)	Sauce Velouté de Poisson	Sauce Velouté de Volaille	Sauce Béchamel	Sauce Hollandaise	Sauce Mayonnaise	Sauce Vinaigrette
Secondary sauce	Demi-Gracé	Velouté		Sauce au Vin Blanc	Sauce Suprême				
Other important derivatives	Bordelaise, Champignons, Charcutière, Chasseur, Diable, Italienne, Lyonnaise, Madère, Périgueux, Piquante, Réforme, Robert, Tortue, Zingara	1. Allemande 2. Câpres, Ciboulette, Estragon, Poulette	Choron, Portugaise, Provençale	Anchois, Bercy, Cardinal, Crevettes, Homard, Joinville, Normande	Chaud-froid	Aurone, Crème, Mornay, Raifort, Soubise	Béarnaise, Choron, Foyot, Maltaise, Mousseline, Riche	Gribiche, Rémoulade, Tartare, Tyrolienne, Verte	Norvégienne, Pecheur, Ravigote

the table. Cherries should likewise be dipped into the water, holding them between the prongs of a fork.

A sugar-shaker should be placed on the table to be available, if required.

Standard sauces etc (hot and cold) from kitchen
The number and types of sauces which will be encountered by waiting staff is legion, and will depend on the type and variety of dishes on the menu, and the frequency that it may be changed. From the point of technical expertise it is best to try and remember them as they are met, rather then to learn lists of sauces that may never be seen.

The majority of sauces met in classic French cuisine for use with meats or fish are based on three main roux-based sauces, and are invariably made by addition of other ingredients to these bases.

The three main roux-based sauces are: Béchamel – a basic white sauce; Espagnole – a basic brown sauce; Velouté – this can be either veal or fish-based.

Apart from the above and their derivatives, there are also butter-based and oil-based sauces, the butter-based being served warm, and the oil-based being served cold.

Sauces are either 'napped' (*nappée*) over meat or fish dishes or sent out to the restaurant in sauce-boats separately (*à part*), in which case they will be served according to section 2.3.11.

Contents and uses of standard sauces
Brown:

Espagnole	– A basic brown sauce. Not usually used on its own.
Demi-Glace	– Refined, concentrated Espagnole. Used mainly as basis for other sauces.
Madère	– Demi-Glacé with the addition of Madeira wine. Used with braised ham, tongue etc.
Bordelaise	– Demi-Glacé with red wine, tarragon, shallots and peppercorns.
Chasseur	– Demi-Glacé with white wine, shallots, tomatoes and mushrooms.
Diable	– Demi-Glacé with white or red wine, shallots, vinegar and Worcestershire sauce.
Italienne	– Duxelles of shallot, onion and mushroom added to a tomatoed Demi-Glacé with white wine and julienne of ham.

Robert	– Demi-Glacé with white wine, onions fried in butter, flavoured with mustard.
Tortue	– Sauce Madére lightly tomatoed, addition of ham stock, paprika and 'turtle herbs'.
Zingara	– Demi-Glacé with reduction of white wine and tomato purée. Additionally julienne of ham, truffles and mushrooms.
Charcutière	– Sauce Robert with addition of julienne, or finely sliced gherkins.
Piquante	– Sauce Diable with chopped gherkins and parsley.
Lyonnaise	– Demi-Glacé with reduction of white wine/wine vinegar, and finely sliced onion.
Perigueux	– Sauce Madère with truffles.
Réforme	– Demi-Glacé and reduction of peppercorns/red wine. Additionally red-currant jelly. Add julienne of truffles, mushrooms, gherkins, tongue and white of hard-boiled egg.
Champignons	– Demi-Glacé with mushrooms, mushroom essence and white wine. (Can also be made with velouté).

Veloute-based

Allemande	– Reduced velouté thickened with egg yolks and cream.
Câpres	– Sauce Allemande with addition of capers. (If for use with fish, use a fish velouté for the Allemande).
Ciboulette	– Sauce Allemande with addition of finely-chopped chives.
Estragon	– Sauce Allemande with addition of finely-chopped tarragon leaves that have been blanched in vinegar.
Poulette	– Sauce Allemande finished with mushroom essence and lemon juice.

Tomato-based

Provençale	– Sauce Tomate with addition of garlic, 'fines herbes', olives, mushrooms, chopped tomatoes, white wine and anchovies pounded with butter.
Choron	– Equal parts of Sauce Tomate and Sauce Béarnaise mixed.

Portugaise	– Sauce Tomate and Veal Velouté with garlic, parsley and chopped fried onion.

Fish-stock-based

Anchois	– Sauce Crème with addition of anchovy butter.
Cardinal	– Béchamel together with lobster butter.
Crevettes	– Fish Velouté with shrimp butter.
Homard	– Sauce Crème with lobster butter and diced lobster.
Joinville	– Sauce Crevettes, with Béchamel and julienne of truffles.
Bercy	– Fish Velouté with shallots and reduction of white wine and fish stock. Finish with chopped parsley.
Normande	– Fish Velouté with mushroom essence and finished with cream.

Chicken-stock-based

Suprème	– Reduced chicken Velouté finished with mushroom essence, cream and lemon juice.
Chaudfroid	– Chicken Velouté. Addition of cream. Beaten and used for coating.

Béchamel-based

Aurore	– Sauce Béchamel with addition of consommé. Reduced and coloured with tomato and cream.
Crème	– Béchamel thickened with yolks of eggs. Finished with double cream and a little lemon juice.
Mornay	– Béchamel thickened with yolks of eggs. Addition of Parmesan and Gruyère cheese. (For flash glazing, as given – for longer glazing omit yolks of eggs) For fish dishes, use fish stock.
Raifort	– Sauce Crème with the addition of grated horse-radish. Finish with lemon juice. (For use hot with boiled beef).
Soubise	– Sauce Béchamel and chicken stock mixed with sweated onion purée.

Butter-based

Hollandaise	– Reduction of shallots, vinegar, butter, salt, cayenne and lemon juice beaten over low heat with egg yolk. Used on its own for vegetables,

	hot prime fish dishes, and as a base, as under.
Béarnaise	– Hollandaise made with tarragon in the vinegar reduction. Finished with chopped tarragon and chervil.
Choron	– Equal quantities of Béarnaise and Tomato Sauce.
Foyot	– Béarnaise with addition of meat glaze.
Maltaise	– Hollandaise with juice and grated zest of blood orange in place of lemon.
Mousseline	– Hollandaise with addition of whipped double cream.
Riche	– Hollandaise with addition of cream, truffle mushrooms and crayfish tails.

Oil-based

Emulsified:

Mayonnaise	– An emulsion of egg yolks, oil, mustard, salt, pepper and lemon juice (or vinegar).
Gribiche	– Thinned mayonnaise with addition of mustard, chopped hard-boiled egg, chopped gherkins, chervil, tarragon, parsley and capers.
Rémoulade	– As gribiche, but without chervil, tarragon or egg.
Tartare	– As gribiche without hard-boiled egg.
Tyrolienne	– Mayonnaise to which is added garlic and shallot sweated in tomato concassée. Finished with chopped parsley.
Verte	– Mayonnaise with addition of blanched, puréed spinach leaves, with chopped parsley and tarragon.

Liquid:

Vinaigrette	– Basically $\frac{2}{3}$ oil and $\frac{1}{3}$ vinegar to which is added some or all of the following: salt, pepper, mustard, finely-chopped onion, parsley, gherkins and capers.
Norvégienne	– Full vinaigrette, with additionally chopped hard-boiled egg yolk and anchovy fillets.
Pêcheur	– Full vinaigrette with the addition of chopped crab meat.
Ravigote	– Full vinaigrette with chopped hard-boiled egg.

Compound butters (Beurres Composés)

In somewhat the same category as sauces; the compound butters are served as adjuncts to various dishes, warm or cold, depending on the dish.

Warm:

Beurre fondu	– melted butter used for asparagus, vegetables, etc.
Beurre noir	– browned butter served as sauce for fish, (notably skate: *Raie au Beurre Noir*), includes lemon juice and parsley.
Beurre noisette	– lightly browned butter with addition of a little lemon juice.
Beurre meunière	– As beurre noisette with chopped parsley.

Cold*:

Beurre à l'ail (Garlic butter)	– Crushed garlic added to butter and pounded together.
Beurre d'Anchois (Anchovy butter)	– butter pounded with anchovy fillets.
Beurre Maître d'Hôtel	– Butter pounded with parsley, salt, pepper, lemon juice.

Note: There are many more butters, most of which are named by their main content, eg Beurre moutarde containing mustard, and Beurre d'Homard containing lobster coral.

Unclassified sauces

Many of these are English in origin and accompany meat dishes, as follows:

Mint Sauce (*Sauce à la Menthe*)	– Chopped mint leaves in sweetened malt vinegar solution. Used for roast lamb.
Cranberry Sauce (*Sauce aux Airelles*)	– Cranberries and sugar as a light jam. Used with roast turkey.
Cumberland Sauce	– Mixture of red-currant jelly, port wine, orange and lemon juice, with mustard, chopped shallots and orange zest. Used for ham, and game pies.
Apple Sauce (*Sauce aux Pommes*)	– Purée of cooking apples, lightly sweetened. Served with roast pork, roast duck, roast goose, etc.
Bread Sauce (*Sauce Pain*)	– Breadcrumbs heated in onion-flavoured milk. Served with roast chicken.

* All the cold butters after compounding are rolled into cylinders about 25 mm in diameter, chilled and then sliced into discs about 7–8 mm in thickness. These are dished on crushed ice and served by the waiters, or, in the case of grills, placed on top in the kitchen.

Proprietary sauces

The use of proprietary sauces is not restricted to popular catering, and they have a place in even the best-class restaurants serving grills, shell-fish etc.

The usual types kept will be a brown sauce such as OK or A1, a tomato ketchup, and Worcestershire sauce, together with Tabasco sauce, for use with shell-fish.

English mustard is usually freshly made daily. French and German mustards, pickles, supplied in jars, should always be kept in good order. The outside of the bottles or jars, together with the necks and inside of the caps must be kept scrupulously clean. They will normally be kept on sideboards, and presented to diners on sideplates with caps off, ready to use, and for pickles, with spoons or pickle forks on the side.

3.2.2.6   Service of wines, spirits, beers and lagers at table

The service of alcoholic beverages, and soft drinks is a specialised task usually performed by the Wine Waiter (*Sommelier*) in a first-class restaurant. However, every waiter should be familiar with the basic service of these drinks.

Wines.   The order for wines is taken after the meal order has been taken and before the first course is served. If separate wines for each course have been ordered, they should be served in a fresh glass, just before each course is served.

As a general rule, red wines are served at room temperature and white and rosé wines are served chilled.

The wine bottle, with the label uppermost, should be presented to the host, and his approval obtained. The capsule covering the top of the neck of the bottle should be cut round, above the 'ledge', then using a cork-screw, the bottle should be un-corked at the table, and a little wine should be poured into the host's glass for testing. On receiving his approval the wine should be poured for all the ladies present then the gentlemen and finally the host himself.

White wines should be left in a wine cooler half-filled with ice and water to the right of the host, and red wine either on a coaster on the table, or in a wine basket, according to the custom of the restaurant.

The glasses should be topped-up periodically until all the wine ordered has been served.

Spirits.   Spirits, with their mixers, are served from the dispense bar. When taking the order for spirits, check with the guest if he would like ice and also his choice of 'mixer'.

Collect the spirit and mixer separately from the bar on a salver. Pour the mixer at the table, so that the guest is able to decide the quantity of 'mixer' required.

Beers and lagers.   Beers and lagers are served from the dispense bar. Some establishments may prefer to open bottled beers and lagers at the table. The waiter should carry the dispensed beers and lagers in their glasses on a salver, and serve them from the right of the guest, placing the glass slightly to the right of the guest.

3.2.2.7   *Preparing and serving of non-alcoholic drinks*

Tea and other infusions.   Tea is produced from the leaves of the tea plant in two main types; 'black' and 'green'. 'Black' tea is produced mainly in India, Pakistan, Bangladesh, Sri Lanka, Kenya, Uganda, Malawi and Mozambique, while 'green' tea comes mainly from China with a little coming from Taiwan (Formosa).

Most teas used in catering are blends prepared by importers or merchants to give the best results for the water of a particular area. Even domestic packet teas sold in different parts of the country will vary because of the different characteristics of the water.

Large leaf teas are the most expensive but on the whole produce a weak liquor and need some time to brew. Over the years British taste has developed a liking for strong, highly coloured brews which can be produced easily from the cheaper grades of teas known as 'fannings' or 'dust', and this in turn has led to the manufacture of tea-bags, in an effort to use these very small-sized teas without leaving particles in the liquor.

Several 'fine' teas having their own characteristics are used in very high-class establishments, but in general it would be a management decision dependent on local acceptability as well as price as to which blend would be used in any given circumstances.

Some of the well-known 'fine' teas include Darjeeling with its rich 'muscatel' flavour, Assam with a strong malty taste, aromatic Ceylon teas, and 'Earl Grey' with its bergamot flavour. Tea should always be made with freshly boiled water, having first warmed the pot, at a rate of one teaspoonful of tea per person, with one extra if using loose tea. If catering tea-bags are used they are obtainable in varying sizes, for making one or more portions, or larger quantities.

Tea should always be stored in cool, dry stores, away from strong-smelling items such as soaps or cheeses, preferably in manufacturers' packing, but quantities bought should not be excessive, as tea does not have an extended 'shelf-life.'

'Black' or Indian teas are usually served (in England) with cold milk and sugar (if desired), the milk being placed first in the cup. Continental guests may wish for cream or warm milk with their tea, and Scottish guests often drink their tea without milk.

'Russian' or lemon tea is served in glasses which are usually held in silver-plated or other metal holders, and is served on a doily-covered side plate, with slices of lemon served separately, and cube sugar.

China tea is traditionally made in a porcelain or earthenware pot and served without milk, but sliced lemon is served, with sugar, as above.

Herbal teas or (*tisanes*) are served in the same manner as China tea and come in different types, being available now either loose or in the form of tea-bags. The usual types are Camomile, Verbena, Lime, Rose-hip and Bergamot, although others are known. Mint tea, made with mint leaves is much appreciated by Arabs and North Africans and is usually served in glasses with sugar, and garnished with a mint leaf.

Iced tea, made with a cold infusion of tea, previously made, is served in glasses with a slice of lemon. Sugar is passed separately.

Note: Tea, unlike coffee is invariably left on the table for guests to help themselves and a jug of hot water is always served with which to correct the strength of the brew to personal taste.

Coffee.   Coffee is an infusion of the ground, roasted beans of the coffee plant (*Coffea Arabica or Coffea Robusta*) and has been known in Europe for some three hundred or more years, having been introduced into Venice in 1615, where a coffee house was established in 1645.

The first coffee house in England was established in Oxford, in 1650, with another in London two years later. Others soon followed, some of which became famous, Jonathan's Coffee House in Change Alley later becoming the London Stock Exchange, and Lloyd's Coffee House in Lombard Street becoming the centre of world insurance, as Lloyd's of London.

Although originally grown in the Yemen, it spread throughout the Arabian area where it was jealously guarded until smuggled out in the sixteenth century. The Dutch started growing coffee in their colonies of Java and Sumatra and Amsterdam became a centre of the coffee trade. The French started to grow it in their colony of Martinique, having been given a plant by the mayor of Amsterdam. Coffee plants were then taken by missionaries to Central and South America and now it is grown in many countries around the world in the area lying between the Tropics of Cancer and Capricorn.

The characteristics of coffee depend on two main factors, the type of coffee bean, and the degree of roasting applied to it.

The robusta type has twice the caffeine content of the arabica and in order to arrive at a standard coffee for any particular purpose, most coffees are blends of differently roasted coffees from different origins.

The different types of roastings are as follows:

Light or pale roastings – Suitable for mild beans to preserve their delicate aroma.

Medium roastings – Give a stronger flavour for coffees with a well-defined character.

Full roastings – These give a bitter flavour, and are favoured in many Latin countries.

High roasted coffee – This strengthens the bitter aspects of the coffee while losing much of the original flavour.

After roasting, which is usually carried out by commercial coffee roasters, the coffee will be sold for grinding, or converted into instant (soluble) coffee.

Roasted coffee beans are normally sold for use in catering outlets either in the bean form, which will require grinding, or already ground, in vacuum packs, usually in a size convenient for use in one of the several types of apparatus described below.

Coffee, when ground, should not be allowed to come into contact with the air, or much of the flavour and essential oils will be lost, and the fineness of the grind will depend on the method of infusion to be used, and the strength desired.

Suppliers will usually supply coffee ground to the fineness specified for the equipment to be used, but the most suitable grinds for the different types of equipment are as follows:

Method	Grinding grade
Filter drip	Fine to medium
Jug	Coarse
Turkish/Greek	Pulverised
Plunger method	Medium
Glass balloon/vacuum/Cona	Medium fine or fine
Espresso	Very fine
Neapolitan	Medium
Percolator	Medium

The London Coffee Information Centre gives the following information on brewing coffee:

'Rules' for making a good cup of coffee:

Water.   Water is added to ground coffee to extract the cell contents and make the brew. A common mistake is to use boiling water. However, this spoils the flavour and aroma of the coffee, and the most satisfactory temperature of the water to make contact with the ground beans is between 92°C and 96°C.

The first step towards a good cup of coffee is to make the brew with fresh cold water which has been boiled and then allowed to cool to this temperature. Automatic coffee machines are normally designed to add water at the ideal temperature.

Coffee.   Once coffee is roasted and then ground it should be used as soon as possible, or stored in airtight containers, in a cool place. Packets or containers usually have some recommendation about the amounts which should be used, and how to make the coffee. In all cases, it is better to be generous with the quantities of coffee used.

The equipment.   Hygiene is vital, and all equipment and utensils should be spotlessly clean.

The Brew.   Coffee always tastes best when freshly brewed. Drink it as soon as possible. It will deteriorate if it is kept too long, and should not be kept for re-heating.

Instant coffee.   Instant coffee is convenient because it can be made into individual cups by adding water to the coffee and stirring. The flavour can be improved if it is made in a pot using about one heaped teaspoon for each cup, according to taste.

The jug.   This is one of the oldest methods of making coffee. If possible, it should be made in a china or earthenware pot, although an enamel pot is also quite suitable.

The pot should be warmed with hot water and dried before adding medium or coarse ground coffee. Water is added and the mixture stirred. It is important to leave the coffee to brew by standing it in a warm place for about five minutes before serving.

The plunger pot.   The plunger pot is a sophisticated version of the jug. It is designed to restrain the coffee grounds when pouring into cups.

The pot consists of a heatproof glass jar which has a plunger with a perforated metal disc which acts as a filter. The coffee is made by using at least four heaped tablespoons of a medium ground coffee to each point of water. The pot should then stand for four to six minutes to brew the coffee before serving.

The automatic drip machine. The maufacturer's instructions should be followed because each make of machine will have some minor variations in operating routine.

Fine ground coffee should be placed into the filter and fresh cold water added to the flask. Once the machine is switched on, it will automatically brew the coffee and keep it hot for serving.

The drip pot. Water which is just off the boil should be poured over the fine ground coffee in the filter until the grounds are wetted. After a minute or so the remaining water can be added. The coffee will then drip through into cup or pot, depending on the size.

Espresso and cappuccino. Espresso machines force steam and water under pressure through coffee grounds. Finely ground, dark roast coffee is used to produce a characteristic, slightly bitter and strong flavour.

Milk, which has been steam heated by means of a steam injector nozzle, is then added to make cappuccino coffee, with, often, a sprinkling of ground chocolate on top.

Vacuum machines. Cold water is poured into a glass bowl which is then twisted into an upper bowl, containing a filter to make an airtight seal.

Medium or fine ground coffee is added to the filter. As the water boils in the lower bowl it rises up the funnel and mixes with the coffee in the upper bowl. This mixture should then be stirred. When the heat is removed from the lower bowl, the coffee will drip down into the lower bowl, ready to serve, after taking off the upper bowl.

Turkish or Greek coffee. Ideally, Turkish or Greek coffee should be made in a traditional long-handled copper container called an 'Ibrik', although a small, narrow and high-sided saucepan can be used. One heaped teaspoon of pulverised dark or continental roast coffee is placed in the Ibrik with each demi-tasse of water.

Turkish or Greek coffee can be drunk without sugar, although if a sweet brew is required, up to one teaspoon of sugar for each spoon of coffee can also be added.

The Plunger Pot (Cafétiere)
Medium ground coffee.
4 heaped tablespoons to 1 pint
water recommended.
Warm pot.
Water just off the boil.
Stir.
Leave.

The Jug
Warm dry pot.
Medium to coarse ground coffee.
Water just off the boil (92–96°C).
Stir. Strain.

Drip Machines
Automatic
Use manufacturers'
instructions.
Fine ground coffee.
Non-Automatic
Fine grind coffee.
Water just off the boil.
Stir before serving.

Glass Cone/
Vacuum Method
Medium grind coffee.

Espresso
Finely ground,
dark roast coffee.

Turkish or
Greek Coffee
Dark roast coffee ground as
finely as possible.
One heaped teaspoon of coffee
to each demi-tasse of water.
Sugar to taste. Bring to boil.
Stir. Remove from heat.
Repeat about 4 times.
Leave to stand.
Pour without straining.

FIG. 3.25 Methods of making coffee (London Coffee Information Centre)

FIG. 3.26 Serving coffee using salver

The mixture should be stirred into the water and brought to the boil. As it boils, it is removed from the heat. This is a ritual which is usually repeated three times. Turkish or Greek coffee should be poured without stirring into very small demi-tasse cups so that each cup contains a little froth.

Milk should never be used.

Service of coffee in the restaurant.   Depending on the type of the establishment, coffee may be served in the restaurant in several ways, as follows:

1. From the flask or cafetière direct into the cup, at the table.
2. Served from coffee pots and milk jugs by the waiter to the diners. Two methods are normally used, either serving from a silver flat which is the accepted 'English' method, or served with a pot in each hand, 'the Continental' method, as shown in Figures 3.26 and 3.27.

Proprietary and other beverages from the Still Room.

Hot Chocolate.   This may be prepared from one of the many proprietary mixes available for this purpose, and will usually entail mixing either a paste or powder with hot or cold milk. If cold milk is used, then it is usually heated by means of a steam injector nozzle

FIG. 3.27 Serving coffee without salver

on the café set. The drink is normally served in an earthenware jug, with a teacup or breakfast cup depending on the time of day. Granulated sugar is also served.

Malted milk.   This is served in the same way as hot chocolate and is usually whisked, using a milk-shake whisk during mixing. The best-known malted milk is Horlicks.

Meat extracts.   The best-known of these are Bovril and Oxo. They are prepared using the requisite amount of the preparation stirred into hot water in a large cup; often special mugs are used bearing the name of the product. Fingers of hot, buttered toast are always served with these beverages, and salt and pepper always passed or placed on the table.

Hot milk.   This is served in the same way as hot chocolate. It is usually best to serve homogenised milk because the cream content does not separate out and therefore will not 'skin' like pasteurised milk.

Cold milk.   This must always be cold, straight from the refrigerator, and will usually be served in a half-pint tumbler placed on a doily-covered side-plate. Cold milk also forms the basis of milk shakes which are cold milk whisked with specially prepared emulsified flavourings made for the purpose and based on fruits, chocolate, coffee etc.

Soft drinks. (ie orange, lemon, lime, syrups and fruit juices.) These days, if a customer requests a fruit squash, either orange, lemon or lime, it is usually prepared from a commercially bottled product and served in a tumbler or Paris goblet, with ice cubes and water or soda water and possibly garnished with a slice of the named fruit together with a straw.

Should the customer desire, and the type of operation permits, then all of the above drinks can be prepared from the fresh fruit, by squeezing the juice, using a glass or other 'squeezer'. The fresh juice must then be strained to remove any pips, fruit debris etc, and then serve, as above.

If juices are ordered they can be prepared by the use of fresh fruit, or more usually by the use of pre-portioned juices supplied in either 'baby' bottles or individual portion cans. For all juices except tomato, caster sugar and a teaspoon is served, with the glass of juice presented on a doily-covered side plate, but for tomato juice, salt and Worcestershire sauce is offered, the service being the same as for fruit juices.

Syrups. These are normally found in the bar for use in mixed drinks and cocktails and the only one that may be encountered in Still-Room service is blackcurrant.

Minerals. Mineral and table waters and other carbonated drinks. Mineral waters are those waters occurring naturally in various countries, some being still and others gassy. The gassy ones all contain carbonic acid (ie carbon dioxide in solution) and this can occur naturally or be artificially introduced.

Because of the content of chemical salts in these waters, many people drink them for their medicinal properties while others drink them from choice, either plain or as mixers with spirits or fruit juices. The best-known mineral waters that may be encountered are as follows:

Contrexeville	France
Evian	France
Perrier	France
Vichy	France
Vittel	France
Ashbourne	UK
Buxton	UK
Malvern	UK
Appollinaris	Germany
San Pellegrino	Italy
Spa	Belgium

Mineral waters, if served alone, are served in Paris goblets, the bottles being left on the table for the diners to help themselves to the remainder. Bottles should always be taken to the table and preferably opened in front of the customer.

Table waters and carbonated drinks are those drinks artificially made which can be drunk on their own, or as mixers with other drinks, such as soda water, ginger ale, ginger beer, tonic water, cola-based drinks, bitter lemon. These will be served as mineral water depending on the size of portion ordered, sometimes as a 'long' drink, and other times as a 'mixer'.

It should be noted that most carbonated drinks sold in Britain are made from mains water, while in some other countries, many of the carbonated drinks are, in fact made with mineral water, and therefore have the same properties as the plain mineral waters.

3.2.2.8 Changing linen in presence of guests

Sometimes it becomes necessary to change table linen in the presence of the guests. The skill is to be able to change the table-cloth without exposing the table-top (which may be stained due to previous spillage etc).
Refer to section 3.1.4, 'clothing tables'.

Table-cloth.
1. Place and unfold the table-cloth as in steps 1 to 12 of the above skill.
2. Drop the bottom fold of new cloth over the far edge of the table.
3. Using fingers 3 and 4 of both hands, grasp the old table cloth.
4. Lay the new table-cloth, as in the basic skill, while pulling out the old cloth from underneath.
5. Check that the new table cloth hangs evenly on all sides. Adjust if necessary.

Slip-cloth. Slip-cloths are smaller than table-cloths, and are used to mask slightly soiled table-cloths during sittings. Another use for slip-cloths is during breakfast or afternoon tea, when coloured cloths may be used.

For the first purpose, slip-cloths may be put on squarely to the table edge as in, Figure 3.28, but some establishments will put on slip-cloths diagonally, irrespective of the purpose.

Method.
1. Stand at one corner of the table facing the opposite corner.
2. Place and unfold the slip-cloth, as for lying a table-cloth, keeping the edges of the table at right angles to the edges of the slip-cloth.

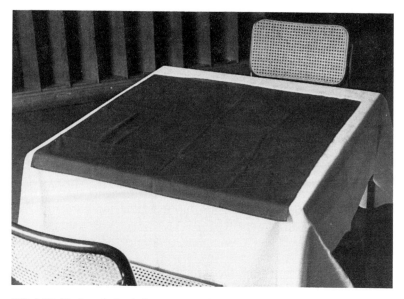

FIG. 3.28 Placing of slip-cloth to cover spills (method 1)

FIG. 3.29 Placing of slip-cloth to cover spills (method 2)

3. The end result is such that only a small triangle of the table-cloth is visible at each corner, keeping these corners equal-sized for good effect, as in Figure 3.29.

3.2.2.9   *Presenting diners' bills*

In first-class establishments the bill should only be presented when asked for. After the coffee has been served, the waiter should look-out for any signs that the diners are ready for their bills. (This also eliminates the need to identify to whom the bill is to be presented.)

Method
1. On being asked for the bill, request it and collect it from the cashier.
2. Check that the bill is correct and that all items have been charged.
3. Unless bill folders are used, fold the bill bringing the top edge to the bottom and turning up the left-hand top corner. If bill folders are used, do not fold.
4. Place folded bill on a side-plate, or unfolded bill into a bill folder.
5. Approach the host from the right and place the side-plate or bill folder to the right of the host. Bills should not be handed to customers.
6. Return to sideboard and wait till payment is placed on the plate or in the folder.
7.*Collect the bill and payment and pay to the cashier.
8. Return receipted bill together with any change due to the customer as in steps 4 and 5.
9. Return to sideboard.

3.2.2.10   *Receiving settlement*

Customers may settle their bills in any one of the following ways: Cash; Cheques; Foreign currency; Travellers' cheques; Credit cards or charge cards; Vouchers; Charge to main bill (in hotels); Charge to credit account/ledger account.

Cash.   This needs no explanation.

Cheques.   Personal bank cheques are normally accepted if accompanied by a valid cheque guarantee card (also known as a banker's card). The present maximum limit of guarantee of such a card is £50. Cheques for amounts over this limit should be referred to management before acceptance.

Note:
* Refer to section 3.2.2.10, 'Receiving settlement' as to various methods of settlement.

Foreign currency. A waiter should familiarise himself with the different foreign currencies acceptable to the establishment, and their rate of exchange.

Travellers' cheques. These are issued by various banking and travel organisations in various currencies and amounts, and bought for cash. They are acceptable at face value when countersigned by the bearer in the presence of the waiter or cashier, but those cheques in foreign currencies are subject to the same rates of exchange.

Credit cards or charge cards. A waiter must be familiar with all the credit cards and charge cards acceptable to the establishment, and must also abide by the vouching procedures set up by the originating companies as to 'floor limits'. Some of the common cards that may be encountered are: Barclaycard (Visa), Access (Mastercharge), American Express, Diner's Club, Carte Blanche.

Vouchers. These are issued by travel agents or airlines, except Luncheon Vouchers (see below). The waiter should always refer the voucher to the cashier for further necessary action.

Luncheon Vouchers. Popular catering establishments accept Luncheon Vouchers at their face value. If the value exceeds the bill no change is given.

Charge to main bill. Customers staying in a hotel may wish their restaurant bill to be charged to their hotel bill. In this case the waiter should obtain the signature of the guest together with his room number on the restaurant bill. Some establishments may ask the guest to show his room key or key card to establish identification.

Charge to credit account or ledger account. This procedure is only permitted by prior arrangement with management and normally a list of those diners permitted to do so will be kept in the restaurant or cash desk. For company accounts, where more than one person may use this facility, a list of those permitted to sign their bills will also be kept.

3.2.2.11   Giving change
Waiting staff should always make to return change to a diner even if the diner has said 'keep the change', especially if a large amount is involved. Should the diner then repeat his request, only then is

it in order to do so, following house rules regarding retention of tips.

3.2.2.12   Accounting for bills

In order to prevent fraudulent mis-use of bills, or acquiring food for personal consumption etc, a strict control of all waiters' bills and other stationery must be exercised.

In those restaurants where a waiter has his own letter or number allocated to him, then the bill books or check pads (KOTs) issued to him will normally be recorded by the head waiter responsible for stationery issue. No spoiled bills may be destroyed, but must be marked 'cancelled' or 'void', and sent in to the cashier with his summary sheet or slip, at the end of the shift.

Likewise, in operations using the 'Continental' system, cashiers must account for every bill used in the same way, marking their summary sheet with both first and last bill numbers, in order to provide a complete financial control and 'audit trail' of all revenue; shown in Figure 3.30.

3.2.3   POST-SERVICE TASKS

Much will depend on several factors, such as whether the restaurant is open for breakfasts, lunches and dinners, and the time of day, as some restaurants will use different linen for breakfast and for lunch.

The general pattern for a day normally starts after the end of the breakfast service, when the whole 'room' is stripped and the mise-en-place for lunch is carried out. The tasks described below are then carried-out, re-laying ready for the service of dinner.

At the end of dinner in a hotel, breakfast will be laid, ready for the morning, but if breakfast is not served in that room, or, in an ordinary restaurant, stripping-down may be done to a greater or lesser degree, depending on the closing time, and time and staff available. No hard and fast rule can be applied.

3.2.3.1   Stripping of tables

At the end of the lunch service, tables should be stripped of all items. If linen colour is not changed for dinner, slip-cloths will be used where necessary, otherwise luncheon-cloths will be left on, in the interest of economy, unless heavily soiled.

3.2.3.2   Returning food items to store, etc

All items of food on sideboards, buffet, trollies, etc, must be returned to the kitchen/service area for proper hygienic storage at the end of the service, and handed over in a proper manner to the person responsible.

The only exceptions to the above are proprietary sauces, mustards etc, which will be cleaned and prepared for the following service in the normal way by the restaurant staff.

3.2.3.3   Stripping sideboards
Between services, sideboards will normally be tidied and replenished with cutlery, crockery, etc., but this will depend on 'house' custom. As above, all food items, water jugs etc will be removed.

3.2.3.4   Cleaning operations
Between lunch and dinner it will normally suffice to move chairs and vacuum beneath tables and in gangways to remove crumbs and other debris, if the floor is carpeted. In a room having a hard floor surface (wood, tiles, etc.) then a soft broom may be used. This should be done before any re-laying of tables is carried out to avoid dust landing on fresh cutlery, plates, etc.

3.2.3.5   Re-clothing of tables
Refer to section 3.2.3.1. Fresh linen will normally only be used where table layouts are to be changed (for parties etc).

Some houses will use coloured slip-cloths for breakfast, which will be placed over the dinner table-cloths, if clean enough.

House rules and customs apply, but it must always be borne in mind that laundry costs rise continually and it is in the interests of everyone that overheads are kept to a minimum so long as the standards of service do not suffer.

3.2.3.6   Re-laying of restaurant
This will be done at the end of the service following house custom, ready for the next meal. It may be completed before staff go off duty, or, if a split duty is worked and staff are on duty during the afternoon, dinner may be laid up by them.

Breakfasts may be laid up in advance by dinner staff before going off duty, or by breakfast staff on arrival.

Should breakfast tables be laid the night before, cups are usually left upside-down, and table-cloths turned up over the covers to prevent the ingress of dust.

4

RELATED BACKGROUND KNOWLEDGE AND INFORMATION

4.1 MENUS

There are mixed opinions as to the origin of menus. Some sources quote the first mention of menus as 1541, when Henry, Duke of Brunswick was seen looking at a list of dishes to be served at a banquet, but the origin is not certain.

While the word 'menu' actually means 'small' or 'detail', it is quite likely that it also comes from the Latin 'minutia' meaning precise or trivial detail.

What is certain is that for centuries the French cooks were given lists known as 'escriteaux' of dishes to be made, which would translate almost exactly to the English 'Bill of Fare'.

Indeed, while the English have adopted the word 'menu', the French use 'la carte' for the equivalent, using the word 'menu' only for a set meal, e.g. Menu @ 40 Fr.

There are two main types of menu configuration in use in classic restaurants, examples of which are shown in Figures 4.1 to 4.10.

4.1.1 TABLE D'HÔTE (FROM THE HOST'S TABLE)

This is a meal of a set number of courses sold at a fixed price, with no reduction for courses not consumed or required. It is also known in French as *'Menu à Prix Fixé'* (Menu at a fixed price). Certain high-cost dishes, if included, may incur an extra charge (*Supplément*).

4.1.2 A LA CARTE (FROM THE MENU (CARD))

Each dish is priced individually, and will usually be prepared or cooked to order, and it is usual for such dishes to have cooking and serving times included on the menu.

Menus of one sort or another are provided for all meals of the day, and may take the form of a card placed in a cover, a wall-board, or the price-list and photographs beloved by the fast-food operators. The aim in all cases is to inform the clientele of what is available, and how much it will cost.

Where applicable, menus will be set out in sections following the order of service of the meal in question, which in the case of luncheon (middle of the day – usually 12–2 pm), and dinner (evening), follows rather loosely the order which has evolved from the French sixteenth- to seventeenth-century custom, and includes some of the titles introduced at that time.

Even up to the end of the eighteenth century, it was customary for a formal meal to be laid out ready on the tables for the diners to come in and eat. This was called the Entrée (entrance). When this 'course' was finished, it was removed and replaced by another series of dishes. This became known as the Relevé (Relieved – or the English equivalent 'remove')

When this second course was finished, the table was cleared (desservie), from which comes the word Dessert.

Before going in to the room in which the meal was to be served, the diners would encounter a series of appetisers in an ante-room which came to be called Hors-d'Oeuvre (ie outside the (main) work).

4.1.2.1   Standard meals and their menus

Breakfast.   The first meal of the day. In hotels and catering outlets two main types of breakfast are recognised. These are known as: Continental breakfast; English breakfast.

The 'Continental breakfast' is a misnomer, being actually the breakfast of France, and exists in two forms *'simple'* and *'complet'* both named after the beverage served eg Thé Simple (tea), or Café Complet (coffee).

The 'simple' form consists only of a large portion of the named beverage.

The 'complet' form consists of the beverage served with French bread or rolls, jam or other preserve and croissants, (crescent-shaped rolls made from flaky, butter-enriched yeast-dough) or brioches (enriched sweetened yeast-dough buns).

In deference to English and American clientele there is usually a supplementary menu containing fruit juice, cereals and egg dishes.

Breakfasts vary in other European countries, with cheese, ham and spiced breads featuring in Holland; and sliced meats, liver sausage etc, with hard-boiled eggs featuring in Germany, all served in addition to the standard 'complet'.

The 'English breakfast' as served in its heyday of Victorian and

Edwardian England was truly a meal in itself, a symbol of the British Empire, large and conservative. In these days of haste and interest in fitness one has neither time nor appetite to eat meals of this magnitude.

Many hotels still present menus containing all or some of the following dishes, and British Rail are still trying to keep up the image of the English breakfast, which consists of the following courses:

Fruit	– Fruit juices (not tomato) or fresh or stewed fruit, (apples, prunes or stewed dried fruit (Compôte de Fruit)).
Cereal	– Porridge served with hot or cold milk, or cream, or a proprietary cereal (corn flakes, muesli etc).
Fish Dishes	– Poached or grilled kippers, bloaters, grilled or fried herrings, poached smoked haddock, deep-fried whiting, or kedgeree.
Egg Dishes	– Boiled, poached, fried, scrambled, coddled, shirred or as omelets.
Meat Dishes	– Grilled or fried bacon or ham; kidneys, grilled or devilled. Rarely nowadays steaks or lamb chops may be offered. Cold buffet meats such as ham, chicken, beef may be served
Vegetables	– Are not usually served for breakfast, except mushrooms, grilled tomatoes, sauté potatoes, or 'bubble and squeak' (fried-over cabbage and mashed potatoes.)

Apart from the above dishes, white and brown bread, rolls, toast and butter are served, together with preserves or honey.

Coffee, tea, chocolate or milk are also served.

Luncheon.   Luncheon or lunch is a meal taken in the middle of the day, usually between noon and 2 pm. The content of the meal will vary with the type of the establishment and/or the wishes of the diners.

Traditionally, the full luncheon menu consisted of some 12 courses, fewer than in a full dinner, but with the dishes being heavier than their dinner counterparts, and included stews, roast joints, grills, cold buffet items, and steamed puddings, both savoury and sweet.

An à la carte luncheon menu will usually contain several choices

Restaurant Panache
Holiday Inn
Bristol

Table d'Hôte Dinner.   Thursday, 15th July.

Soup du Jour, or, Pâté de Campagne,
   or, Florida Cocktail.

Best End of Lamb 'Persilliade':- £7.75.
or, Coq au Vin :- £7.75.
or, Fried Goujons of Sole :- £7.75.
or, A Selection of Cold Cuts with Salad :- £8.25.
or, Prime Roast Ribs of Beef from the Trolley :- £10.25.
(all served with a choice of Vegetables, Potatoes, or a Salad.)

Sweet Course from the Trolley.
or, Cheese & Biscuits.

Coffee.

The price of the Menu is shown against the
selected Main Course, and includes V.A.T.
        (Gratuities are at your discretion.)

FIG. 4.1 Menu – Table d'Hôte

our commencer

Poire d'avocat choisie £2.85
Avocado pear served with prawns and garlic mayonnaise, crabmeat or tarragon vinaigrette.

Melon frappé des glaciers £2.45
Seasonal melon, served with orange sorbet, port or plain with candied ginger.

Saumon d'Ecosse fumé au citron £4.70
Freshly cut Scotch smoked salmon served with lemon and wholemeal bread.

Pâté de gibier en croûte sauce Cumberland £2.50
Venison game pâté cooked in pastry and served with an orange and Port sauce.

Les petits bonnets du midi £2.25
Fresh button mushrooms sauteed with white wine and fine herbs.

Mesclum de fettucine carbonara £2.25
Fresh green noodles blended with diced onions, served with ham and cream.

Mille feuilles d'escargots Marseillaise £4.50
A combination of snails, strips of oxtongue, walnuts flamed with Pernod, served on a bed of spinach and sealed with puff pastry.

es potages

Consommé brunoise au madère £1.45
Golden beef consommé garnished with vegetables and madeira.

Crème de volaille aux pointes d'asperges £1.55
Cream of chicken soup with asparagus tips, chives and cream.

es poissons et crustacés

Queues de scampis du vieux port   £6.25
Lightly pan fried scampis garnished with crabmeat and pimentos, served with a cheese and sherry sauce.

Plat special du bord de mer   £5.95
"Mixed grill" of salmon, halibut, sole, scallops and lotte served with garlic butter and lemon.

Sole grillée belle meunière   £6.45 or £5.95
Grilled lemon sole, garnished with mushrooms, tomatoes, almonds and asparagus tips, served with roe and lemon butter or served plain grilled with lemon.

Grenouilles en croûte à la
mousse verte   £5.75
Frogs legs wrapped in a pastry case and served with a mushroom and watercress sauce.

es entrées

Carré d'agneau persillade   £6.50

Roast best end of lamb served with herbs and garlic, garnished with grilled tomato, gaufrette potatoes and watercress.

Escalope de veau vieille Angleterre   £7.75
Veal escalope filled with stilton cheese and nuts, served with a Madeira sauce.

Suprême de volaille côte de Provence   £5.75
Breast of chicken garnished with ratatouille and served with a light cheese sauce.

Mignon de boeuf au poivre des îles   £9.25
Pan fried end fillet of beef, studded with peppercorn,
flamed with brandy, served with mushrooms, shallots and
tomato sauce.

Cassolette de caneton
"Aux Primeurs"   £6.75
Duckling gently cooked in honey and cider, served with a
garnish of fresh vegetables.

"Our maître d'hôtel will be pleased to offer you a choice of
fresh seasonal foods purchased from local markets."

De l'etal du boucher
All our steaks are cut from prime Scotch beef.

Entrecôte grillée au cresson   £7.90
Centre cut from the prime sirloin of beef. Grilled to your
liking served with traditional garnishes.

Coeur de fillet sauce Béarnaise   £10.50
Grilled fillet of beef served with gaufrette potatoes and
Béarnaise sauce.

Brochette de porc aux champignons   £6.75
Marinated pork fillets grilled on a skewer, served on a bed of
rice with a mushroom and Madeira sauce.

From the silver trolley

Côte de boeuf rôtie sauce Raifort   £7.50
A generous cut from roasted rib of beef, served with
horseradish sauce, Yorkshire pudding, watercress.

All prices include VAT
Gratuities are at your discretion.

Les légumes

Bouquetière de légumes de saison   £1.90
A selection of seasonal vegetables.

Pommes de terre frites, au four,
croquette et du jour   £0.85

Salade du Patron   £2.50
A salad niçoise with chef's special dressing.

Salades de saison   £1.55
Our selection from salads in season.

Les desserts

                                                 £1.60
Please select your choice from the sweet trolley and from
our range of ice creams.

Pour terminer

Plateau de fromages   £1.60
A selection of English and Continental cheese served with
walnut bread and biscuits.

Café

Served with Holiday Inn chocolate mints   £0.70

Café Gaelic, with Irish whiskey; Caribbean with
Jamaica rum; Royal with brandy.

All priced at   £1.70

FIG. 4.2 Menu – À la Carte

Good Morning

The English Breakfast £5.80

Orange or Prune or Tomato Juice
or Porridge or Cold Cereals with Cream or Milk
or Chilled Grapefruit

Your choice of eggs served with
Ham, Bacon, Sausages or Mushrooms
or
Scotch Kippers

Crescents, Breakfast Rolls or Toast
with
Butter, Marmalade, Jam and Honey

Pot of Tea, Coffee, Chocolate or Milk

The Continental £3.40

Orange or Prune or Tomato Juice
or Chilled Grapefruit

Crescents, Breakfast Rolls or Toast
with
Butter, Marmalade, Jam and Honey

Pot of Tea, Coffee, Chocolate or Milk

A La Carte

Fruits & Juices

Orange or Grapefruit Juice   £0.65
Large Juice   £1.25
Tomato or Prune Juice   £0.65
Chilled Grapefruit   £0.65
Sliced Banana with Cream   £1.00
Fresh Fruit Salad   £1.95   Stewed Prunes   £1.10
Sliced Oranges £1.10   Ice Melon from £3.80 (in Season)
Fresh Strawberries   from £3.20 (in Season)

Scrambled Egg   £2.55
Porridge or Cold Cereals with Cream or Milk   £1.00
Cold Cereals with Sliced Bananas   £1.55
Boiled Eggs prepared to your wish: one £1.00 two £1.95
Eggs with Bacon or Sausages £2.55 with Ham £3.20
Omelettes Plain or Fines Herbes £4.40 with Ham £4.60
Bacon, Mushrooms or Pork Sausages £1.25 Ham £2.55
Griddle Cakes with Maple Syrup   £1.95
Breakfast Sirloin Steak   £6.30
Scotch Kippers, the pair   £3.20
Grilled Ham Steak   £6.30
Order of Rolls, Toast, Butter and Honey
Jam or Marmalade   £2.20
Order of Cheese £1.95   Cold Ham or Salami £5.00

Beverages

Coffee £0.80   Pot of Tea (India or China) £0.80
Hot Chocolate £0.80   Cocoa £0.80
Fresh Milk £0.80   Yoghurt £0.80
Infusions £0.80

**The above Prices are inclusive of Government Tax
and Service Charge.**

FIG. 4.3 Menu – Breakfast

English Afternoon Tea
£6.95

A selection of freshly cut sandwiches

Toasted English Muffin

Scones with Jam and
Devon Clotted Cream

Fruit Cake

A Choice of French Pastries or Gâteaux

Balijen Indian Tea

Lapsang Souchong China Tea

Waldorf Special Blend Tea

Served from 3.30 – 6. 30 p.m.
Price includes Service and V.A.T.

FIG. 4.4 Menu – Afternoon Tea

AFTERNOON TEA MENU

BEVERAGES

A pot of Indian or China Tea,
   per person
A pot of Coffee
Cup of Coffee
Cup of Black Coffee and Cream
Glass of Milk
Horlicks or Chocolate
Minerals and Chocolate
Orange or Lemon Squash

BUNS AND CAKES

Assorted Continental Pastries

Danish Pastry

Continental Gateaux or Torte

Fruit or Madeira Cake

Bath Bun

Biscuits

Chocolate Biscuits

BREAD, TOAST, etc.

White Bread and Butter
Brown Bread and Butter
Buttered Toast
Toasted Buttered Scone or Bun
Crispbread
Butter, per pat
Jam or Honey

SANDWICHES

Smoked Salmon

Chicken

Ham or Tongue

Egg and Cress

Cheese

WAFFLES

with
   Jam and Dairy Cream
with
   Maple Syrup or Sauce

OMELETTES

Nature
Ham
Cheese
Mushroom

COLD BUFFET

Wing of Chicken with Ham or
   Tongue and Mixed Salad
Egg Mayonnaise
Ham with Salad
Tongue with Salad
Veal, Ham and Egg Pie and Salad
Home Made Mayonnaise

SAVOURIES

Mushrooms on Toast

Poached Egg on Toast

Welsh Rarebit

Buck Rarebit

FIG. 4.5 Menu – High Tea

SPECIAL TEAS

No. 1 Egg Benedictine
Poached Egg on Ham and Toasted
Muffin with Cheese Sauce, Pot of
Tea and Pastry

No. 2

Grilled Ham and Eggs (2), Bread and
Butter, Pastry, Pot of Tea

No. 3
Home-made Scones with Dairy Cream
and Jam, Pot of Tea

No. 4 Buck Rarebit
(Poached Egg on Welsh Rarebit), Pot
of Tea and Pastry

FISH

Fried Fillet of Plaice, Fried Potatoes

GRILLS *(15 minutes)*

Fillet steak (when available) with choice of vegetables

Rump Steak, Tomatoes, Mushrooms, Garden Peas and Fried Potatoes

Mixed Grill (Cutlet, Sausage, Bacon, Tomato and Mushrooms with Fried
Potatoes)

Grilled Lamb Cutlets (2) with Tomatoes and Fried Potatoes

COLD SWEETS

Fruit Salad and Cream

Crême Caramel

Fresh Chocolate Mousse

Meringue Chantilly

ICE CREAM AND SUNDAES

Vanilla

Strawberry

Caramel Fudge, per portion

Knickerbocker Glory

Peach Melba

Coffee

Chocolate

Walnuts, per portion

Banana Split

Meringue Glacé

Le Diner

Le Pâté aux Herbes
A delicate terrine of ham and veal, flavoured with herbs

ou

Les Quenelles de Sole Newburg
Quenelles of sole served with a delicate lobster sauce

ou

La Petite Marmite
A rich consommé garnished with vegetables and served with croutons

—◎—

Le Filet de Saumon au Champagne
Fillet of salmon poached in champagne and laced with cream

ou

Les Noisettes d'Agneau Celestine
Tender fillets of lamb marinated in lemon juice, gently fried
and served in a stilton and port sauce

ou

Les Cotelettes de Veau aux Chanterelles
Cutlets of veal, filled with pâté de foie gras, gently braised and
served with a wild mushroom sauce

All dishes are accompanied with a selection of vegetables

FIG. 4.6 Menu – Dinner

Le Sorbet aux Framboises et Melon Printanier
Raspberry sorbet and melon cocktail served on crushed ice

ou

La Delice aux Dames

Le Café

£12.50
Price inclusive of Service and Value Added Tax,
however if you believe you have received exceptional service,
please feel free to reward the staff accordingly.

The Cavendish Restaurant

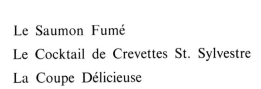

Le Saumon Fumé

Le Cocktail de Crevettes St. Sylvestre

La Coupe Délicieuse

 ★

Le Consommé de Tortue au Sherry

Les Paillettes Dorées

 ★

Le Suprême de Sole Excellence

 ★

Le Blanc de Poulardine Sans Soucis

Les Haricots Verts Maître d'Hôtel

Les Pommes Boutons d'Or

 ★

La Doyenne du Comice Bonne Année

Le Désir des Dames

FIG. 4.7 Menu – Supper

in each course, while a good table d'hôte menu will include at least two choices of some 3 to 5 courses.

Courses offered for luncheon are as follows:

Hors-d'Oeuvre	– Though labelled as hors-d'oeuvre which are various highly-seasoned meat, fish or salad items served singly, or as a selection, the title includes those substitutes such as melon, fruit cocktails, and fruit juices, as well as vegetables such as corn-on-the-cob, artichoke and asparagus.
Soups (*Potages*)	– Thick or clear, including such soups as Scotch Broth and Minestrone.
Farinaceous (*Farineux*)	– Including all pasta dishes, savoury rice dishes, gnocchi, etc.
Egg Dishes (*Oeufs*)	– All methods of preparation except boiled.
Fish (*Poissons*)	– Steamed, poached, grilled and fried (deep and shallow) with simple garnishes. Hot shellfish dishes such as scallops or mussels but not lobster, except in speciality restaurants.
Meat Dishes (*Viandes*)	– These will usually be taken from one or more of the following types:
Entrées	– Made-up meat dishes such as boiled, braised or stewed meats, offal etc, and réchauffé dishes.
Roasts (*Rôtis*)	– Butcher's meat rather than poultry and game.
Grills (*Grillades*)	– Butcher's meat and chicken with plain garnish.
Cold Buffet (*Buffet Froid*)	– Usually cold roasts of either butcher's meat or poultry, or pies, etc, with accompanying salads.
Vegetables (*Légumes*, (*Entremets de*))	– Served as separate course, this would consist of a high-class vegetable such as asparagus (hot or cold), globe artichokes, or corn-on-the-cob.

Soufflés (savoury)	– Can be made from cheese, ham, mushrooms game, etc. Rarely served at this stage of a meal nowadays. More usually served as an hors-d'oeuvre substitute.
Sweet Course (*Entremets* (*Doux*))	– May be any one of the innumerable types of sweet dish from the lightest creams and fools to steamed puddings, pastries, cakes, fritters, etc.
Cheese (*Fromages*)	– Any of the many different cheeses served with biscuits, rolls or French bread with butter, together with celery, radishes, watercress or apples, according to diners' wishes.
Dessert	– Fresh fruit and nuts.
Coffee (*Café*)	

Tea.   Tea as a 'meal' is a British invention and has been accepted even in France. While afternoon tea is usually served in Britain at 4 pm, it had become known in France as 'le five o'clock'.

The meal as opposed to the beverage has evolved into three main types:

Afternoon tea –	This consists of dainty, crustless sandwiches, often of cress or cucumber, together with thin brown bread and butter, jam or honey, sliced fruit cake or pastries and tea, either Indian or China.
Cream teas –	A variation of afternoon tea originating in Devon or Cornwall consisting of freshly-baked scones, jam and clotted cream, together with cakes or pastries, and tea.
High tea –	Originating in Scotland and the North of England, it consists of a choice of fish, meat or egg dishes fried or sauté potatoes, white bread and butter, and often Scotch pancakes (pikelets), fruit or other tea-breads, jam, cakes and tea.

Dinner.   The full traditional dinner menu comprising some 12 to 14 courses is rarely, if ever served to-day, except perhaps at State banquets. An elaborate meal, it included some of the dishes served at luncheon, with some others, but the courses had a much lighter 'accent' than those of luncheon. The courses served traditionally were as follows:

Soup	(*Potage*)
Fish	(*Poisson*)
Entrée	(*Entrée*)
Relevé	(*Relevé*)
Sorbet	(*Sorbet*)
Roast	(*Rôti*)
Salad	(*Salade*)
Cold Dish	(*Mets Froid*)
Vegetable	*Légumes*, (*Entremet de*)
Sweet	(*Entremet*) (*Doux*)
Savoury	(*Savoureux*)
Dessert	(*Dessert*)
Coffee	(*Café*)

At less formal dinners a cheese course might have been introduced between the savoury and dessert. Hors-d'oeuvre were not usually included, but a recent trend had been to include those individual hors-d'oeuvre substitutes, such as oysters, smoked salmon, trout and frogs' legs. Hors-d'oeuvre variés are not used for a classic dinner menu.

Soups	– Choice of clear or thick, including consommé en gelée and tortue claire. The only 'broth' type soup served would be petite marmite.
Fish	– Poached prime fish; salmon, trout, turbot etc garnished and sauced in classical fashion.
	– Fried (deep): whitebait, scampi, fillets in goujons. (shallow): prime fish cooked à la meunière.
	– Grilled: salmon, sole, turbot, red mullet.
	– Cold, in aspic: salmon, sole, trout, salmon trout. Shellfish: all hot styles (except mussels).
Entrées	– Lighter than at lunch, with no vegetables, if followed by a relevé.

Would include vols au vent, hot mousses, kidneys, sweetbreads, cutlets and cuts from fillet sauté, fried and sauté chicken, etc.

Relevé — Dishes of butcher's meat needing carving (Poêlé not roast), or chicken (en casserole, poêlé, etc) garnished as below. Braised ham, tongue, duck, or feathered game, garnished with vegetable other than cabbage or root vegetables, eg celery or artichoke bottoms; and fine potato dishes such as Pommes Anna, Pommes cocotte, Pommes château, but not Pommes purée or Pommes frites.

Sorbet — A water or light sherbet ice flavoured with fruit liqueur or champagne. Originally served with Russian cigarettes as a 'refresher' to the palate during a long formal meal.

Roast (*Rôti*) — Butcher's meat is never served except possibly fillet of beef. The normal roast is either feathered game and poultry, hare or venison.

Salad (*Salade*) — Salads served are plain eg green etc, or compound salad (*salade composée, eg salade Mimosa, salade japonaise*).

Cold Dish (*Mets Froid*) — Cold fish or meat mousses (salmon, ham etc); Foie gras, Aspics, Pâtés, Terrines, timbales, soufflés, etc.

Vegetable ((*Entremet de*) *Légumes*) — A fine vegetable capable of being served on its own, such as globe artichoke, asparagus, aubergine, seakale, or truffles.

Sweet (*Entremet (Doux)*) — Hot and cold soufflés, pancakes, filled or flambées, all types of ice-cream dishes, (served with 'friandises' or petits fours, and fruit-based dishes, such as condés, créoles etc.)

Savoury (*Savoureux*)	– All types, usually based on toast, or tartlets. Highly-seasoned, with cheese, fish, mushrooms, etc.
Dessert	– All fresh fruit and dried fruit, such as Valencia raisins, dates, figs and nuts.
Coffee (*Café*)	– All types of coffee possible; normal, liqueur, Turkish etc, often served with petits fours (if not served with the sweet course), or after-dinner mints, etc.

Supper (Souper). Supper menus, as such are rarely found nowadays, and this meal found its popularity in the days when people went to the theatre after a snack or light meal without taking dinner, and supper was taken before the journey home.

Supper menus are now only seen as a speciality in those hotels and restaurants situated in Central London near to the majority of the theatres, although now most hotels having 'coffee shops', even this trend has almost disappeared.

Menus are of the Table d'Hôte type and consist of some three courses with several dishes being in general of the type served for dinner menus, but with the addition of grills similar to those served at lunch, and for establishments serving after midnight and during the early hours of the morning, breakfast dishes such as kippers, and bacon and eggs also appear.

4.1.3   MENU TERMINOLOGY

Whether to use French or vernacular terms in writing menus is a subject over which much discussion has taken place.

There are arguments for putting menus into English but the authors contend that the use of French is no more than a 'shorthand' which avoids much description.

Basically, whatever language is used, a diner wishes to know two facts: What he is going to eat; How it will be cooked.

This is fine if one keeps to simple things or whole items such as the smaller fish (eg herring, trout), one of which would constitute a portion.

As soon as one tackles the problem with, say, larger fish which need cutting-up or joints of meat, then another factor must be considered and that is the cut.

FOR THANKSGIVING AT PLYMOUTH IN THE BAY COLONY

NOVEMBER 24, 1623, A.D.

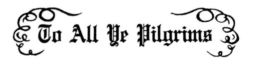

Inasmuch as the great Father has given us this year an abundant harvest of Indian corn, wheat, beans, squashes, and garden vegetables, and has made the forests to abound with game and the sea with fish and clams, and inasmuch as He has protected us from the ravages of the savages, has spared us from pestilence and disease, has granted us freedom to worship God according to the dictates of our own conscience; now, I, your magistrate, do proclaim that all ye Pilgrims, with your wives and little ones, do gather at ye meeting house, on ye hill, between the hours of 9 and 12 in the day time, on Thursday, November ye 29th of the year of our Lord one thousand six hundred and twenty three, and the third year since ye Pilgrims landed on ye Pilgrim Roch, there to listen to ye pastor, and render thanksgiving to ye Almighty God for all His blessings.

WILLIAM BRADFORD
Y_e Governor of Y_e Colony

Ye Bill of Thanksgiving Fare

To Begin the Feaste

An Appetite Whetter

Chopped Chicken Livers on a Bed of Lettuce
Fall Melon from the Patch

FIG. 4.8 Menu – Banqueting/Function

And then a Soup

The Clam Chowder of New England   An Herb Soup of Split Peas

A Salad of Tossed Greens

Followed by The Main Course

Roasted Tom Turkey from the Scullery, with a Sauce of Cranberries
and a Dressing of Celery

And From the Community's Gardens

Sweet Potatoes that are Candied

Yellow Corn Kernels in Cream from the Hull   Buttered Sprouts from the Harvest

Accompaniments from the Baking Ovens

An Abundance of Corn Bread, Pecan Rolls and Rye Bread

To Compleat the Feaste

Golden Harvest Pumpkin Pie   A Pie of Apples and Mincemeat

Coffee from the Indies   Tea from Auld England

Seventeen Pounds Fifty Pence

Inclusive of Service and V.A.T.

*Ye Rib Room in Ye Carlton Tower Hotel Situated in the Royal Borough of Kensington and Chelsea
in the City of London*

The Garden Café

Menu

Appetisers

Chilled fruit juice (apple, grapefruit, orange, pineapple or tomato) 50p

Melon £1.75   Grilled grapefruit 80p   Mushrooms in cider £1.10

Prawn Medley £2.05   Smoked salmon £3.65   with scrambled egg £4.65

Pâté selection (chicken liver, mixed herb or kipper) £1.25

Hot: Seafood Timbale £1.75   Beef skewer (served with an oriental peanut butter sauce) £1.95

Soups

Freshly made soup of the day 75p

Goulash soup 75p   as a main course with garlic french bread £1.25

Egg & Pasta Dishes

The White House bacon and egg plate £2.50

Omelettes: plain £1.75; your choice £2.00   Tagliatelle £2.55   Vegetarian casserole £2.10

Winnsborough Beans (a pot of beans in a chilli and tomato sauce) £2.55

Salad Specialities

Devilled ham rolls £3.50   Chef's salad £4.95
(served on a bed of crisp salad)   (a combination of chicken, smoked salmon and assorted salads)

The country meat plate £3.50
(a choice of beef, chicken or ham with celery, tomato, spring onion and wholemeal bread)

Quiche and salad £3.25   Low calorie salad £3.25
(a selection of quiches available)   (tuna fish and cottage cheese)

Fish

Baked cod £3.55
(with mushrooms, onions and duchess potatoes)

Goujons of plaice £3.85   Grilled lemon sole £4.65
(with french fries)   (with french fried potatoes)

FIG. 4.9 Menu – Coffee Shop

Entrées

Sirloin steak £5.70
(with mushrooms and baked potatoes)

Park Schnitzel Holstein £4.75
(with croquette potatoes)

Grilled spring chicken £4.65
(with rosemary butter croquette potatoes)

Lamb kebabs £4.75
(with oriental rice)

Chicken & ham pie £4.65
(with parsley potatoes)

Veal piccata £4.75
(served on a bed
of buttered spaghetti)

12oz T-Bone steak £6.75
(with mushrooms, onion rings and
french fried potatoes)

Vegetables of the day or salads 65p

Hamburgers

American-style chopped pure beef chargrilled hamburgers
served with french fried potatoes and relishes

Hamburger: 4oz £2.50;   8oz £3.95

Eggburger (4oz burger with a fried egg, and fried onion rings) £2.80

Blue Cheese Burger (4oz burger topped with melted blue cheese) £2.85

Dish of the Day

<u>30th June 1983</u>

Orange and Carrot Soup £0.75p

Turkey Escalope in Mexican Sauce served with New
Potatoes and Buttered Broccoli £3.10p

Buttered Mixed Vegetables £0.65p

Sandwiches

Served on brown, white or toasted bread

A selection of freshly-made sandwiches   from £1.60

Prawn & egg open sandwich £2.20

Albany "double-decker" club £2.95   Welsh Rarebit £2.15

Mice & Men £2.20
(asparagus & tomatoes topped with melted cheese)

Desserts

Please refer to Dessert Menu

Beverages

Coffee: White House high roast or decaffeinated (with milk or cream) 50p

The Garden Café coffee special (a mug of coffee with whipped cream, nutmeg and a chocolate flake) 70p

Expresso/Capuccino 55p   Pot of tea 50p   Hot chocolate with whipped cream 60p

Lemon tea 50p   Cold milk 45p   Milk shakes (vanilla, chocolate, raspberry or strawberry) 75p

All prices are inclusive of 15% VAT and gratuities are at guests' discretion.

Welcome to your Berni Inn.

We hope you enjoy your meal. Why not try some of our famous draught sherry, as an aperitif?

Dry Fino Sherry	Glass 38p	Schooner 50p
Bristol Milk Sherry	Glass 38p	Schooner 50p

Chilled Fruit Juice or Tomato Juice 26p

Starters: Soup 46p   Pâté 91p   Prawn Cocktail 96p

8oz Prime Sirloin Steak

Grilled to your liking and served with french fried
potatoes or baked jacket potato with sour cream
and chives, garden peas, tomato, roll and butter.
And to follow, ice cream, or a selection of cheese
and biscuits.   £4.48

8oz Prime Rump Steak

Grilled to your liking and served with french fried
potatoes or baked jacket potato with sour cream
and chives, garden peas, tomato, roll and butter.
And to follow, ice cream, or a selection of cheese
and biscuits.   £4.30

12oz Prime T-Bone Steak

Grilled to your liking and served with french fried
potatoes or baked jacket potato with sour cream
and chives, garden peas, tomato, roll and butter.
And to follow, ice cream, or a selection of cheese
and biscuits.   £5.90

8oz Prime Fillet Steak

Grilled to your liking and served with french fried
potatoes or baked jacket potato with sour cream
and chives, garden peas, tomato, roll and butter.
And to follow, ice cream, or a selection of cheese
and biscuits.   £5.98

6oz Gammon Steak with Fried Egg or Pineapple

Grilled and served with french fried potatoes or
baked jacket potato with sour cream and chives,
garden peas, tomato, roll and butter. And to
follow, ice cream, or a selection of cheese and
biscuits.   £2.96

FIG. 4.10 Menu – Fast Food

Half a Chicken

Oven roasted and served with barbecue sauce, french fried potatoes or baked jacket potato with sour cream and chives, garden peas, tomato, roll and butter. And to follow, ice cream, or a selection of cheese and biscuits.

£3.16

Half a Duckling

Oven roasted and served with orange or apple sauce, french fried potatoes or baked jacket potato with sour cream and chives, garden peas, tomato, roll and butter. And to follow, ice cream, or a selection of cheese and biscuits.

£5.16

8ozs Fillets of Plaice

Deep fried and served with tartare sauce, lemon, french fried potatoes or baked jacket potato with sour cream and chives, garden peas, roll and butter. And to follow, ice cream, or a selection of cheese and biscuits.

£3.08

Scampi

Deep fried and served with tartare sauce, lemon, french fried potatoes or baked jacket potato with sour cream and chives, garden peas, roll and butter. And to follow, ice cream, or a selection of cheese and biscuits.

£4.44

◄●►
The Berni Salad 53p extra
◄●►
Alternative Sweets:

Cheesecake 50p   Gâteau 50p
Dutch Apple Pie and Cream 50p

All items are subject to availability, and the weights shown are approximate weights before cooking. The ice cream contains non-milk fat.

All our prices include VAT.
There is no service charge.   Gratuities are at the discretion of the customer.

Please talk to the Manager if you have any helpful suggestions arising from your visit. If you cannot do this, write to the Managing Director, Berni Inns Ltd., The Pithay, Bristol BS99 7BW.

681M3

By the glass

French Red, White or Rosé   70p

French Table Wine

		BOTTLE	HALF
1.	Red	£3.47	—
2.	White	£3.47	—
3.	Rosé	£3.47	—

Yugoslavian

4.	Laski Riesling	£3.75	£2.04

French

5.	Bordeaux AOC, (Red)	£4.62	£2.55
6.	Beaujolais AOC, (Red)	£4.62	£2.55
7.	Côtes du Rhône AOC, (Red)	£4.62	£2.55
8.	Muscadet AOC, (White)	£4.10	£2.28
9.	Anjou Rosé AOC	£4.46	£2.37
10.	Champagne NV	£7.84	£4.27
11.	Châteauneuf-du-Pape AOC, (Red)	£5.95	£3.15

German

12.	Liebfraumilch QbA	£4.62	£2.55
13.	Moselle QbA	£4.62	£2.55

Italian

14.	Chiänti DOC, (Red)	£5.23	£2.70
15.	Asti Spumante DOC	£5.80	£3.14

AOC — Appellation d'Origine Contrôlée — French
QbA — Qualitätswein — German
DOC — Denominazione di Origine Controllata — Italian

All items subject to availability and prices include VAT.

Enjoy a freshly made coffee or liqueur coffee at the bars.

WL1

Human nature being what it is, man is never satisfied with the simple things, and over the centuries, national, regional, local and personal variations have crept in, leading to a style or garnish-title.

For simple 'roast beef', the 'what' and 'how' has thus become: Contrefilet de boeuf rôti à l'Anglaise (Roast sirloin of beef, English style)

CUT   WHAT HOW STYLE

and even if one translates this into English, the 'man in the street' still has to know what a sirloin is, and that 'English style' (in this context only) indicates the presence of Yorkshire pudding, roast gravy, and horseradish sauce.

Names of foodstuffs in common use are given in the text and other terms follow after section 4.1.3.1, 'Methods of cookery' below.

The 'how' are all methods of cooking, and the past participle of the verb in question is used (eg to fry = fried).

4.1.3.1 Methods of cookery

Boiling (Bouillir – Bouillie(e)). The process of cooking food immersed in a liquid (usually water). Used for cooking vegetables, and for pickled meats.

Poaching (Pocher – Poché(e)). The process of simmering in a liquid, which is usually stock or a mixture of water and vinegar, with spices, or even in milk. The process seals the flavour inside the coating of albumen that is caused during the process, but if allowed to boil instead, then toughening of the foodstuff ensues.

Roasting (Rôtir – Rôti(e)). The process of cooking food items in the oven, dry except for sufficient fat to stop the item sticking to the pan (if used). Technically, roasting should be done above or in front of an open fire (as on a spit) rather than in an enclosed oven. Food items are not covered. A high temperature is often used with meat to seal it initially, after which the heat is reduced, to avoid shrinkage.

Braising (braiser – Braisé(e)). Used for joints of meat. As roasting, but the meat is cooked after sealing in a hot pan on a bed of root vegetables (*mirepoix*) with a liquor of water or water and wine, etc and cooking is effected in a covered pan.

Grilling (Griller – Grillé(e)).   Cooking process used for small prime cuts such as steaks, chops, etc, or small fish. Similar to roasting process, but heat transfer is effected through contact with hot metal grill plate or bars. Heat should be from below, but many establishments use a top-heat grill, which is technically not a grill, but a salamander.

Frying (Frire – Frit(e)).   The process of cooking by immersion in hot fat or oil. Two distinct types of frying are practised:

Deep frying   – used for fish or meats which have been coated with batter or egged and bread-crumbed; or fried potatoes, etc.

Shallow frying   – used for fish which has been floured only, such as for meunière (qv), or collops (*escalopes*), ie thin cuts of butcher's meat or poultry, which have been coated with egg and breadcrumbs as protection, but need little cooking.

Pot-roasting (Poêler – Poêlé(e)).   Process similar to braising, but almost dry, using just a minimal amount of liquor.

Sauté (Sauter – Sauté(e)).   A process of light frying in an almost-dry pan. So called, because the food is kept on the move by shaking the pan (sauter means to jump).

Terms used for degrees of cooking.   Mainly for grills (steaks etc):

Very underdone (flared, seared or rare)	Bleu(e)
Underdone	saignant(e)
Medium cooked ('done to a turn')	à point
Well-done	bien cuit(e)

Other menu terms denoting procedures

en Barquette	in a boat-shaped mould.
Bouchée(s)	a small puff-pastry case filled with a savoury mixture (lit 'a mouthful').
à la Broche	cooked on a spit.
Brochette de	food cooked on a skewer (as a 'kebab').
Brouillés	scrambled, as of eggs.
à Cheval	on a slice of toast etc (lit 'on horseback').
en Cocotte	cooked in a ramekin.
Confit de	a confection (usually refers to goose liver).

à la Coque	boiled in the shell, as of eggs.
en Coquille	served in a shell, usually a scallop shell, or other.
Cromesqui(s)	a cork-shaped rissole, usually of cooked meat.
Croquette(s) de	a cork-shaped deep-fried potato dish.
Croustade de	a pie, usually of game.
en Croûte	in a pastry case, usually of meat, or game.
sur Croûte	on a slice of toast.
cru(e)	raw.
Crudités	a selection of raw vegetables, served as an hor-d'oeuvre.
Diablé(e)	devilled, usually containing cayenne pepper.
Emincé de	thin slices of meats (does not mean minced).
Farci(e) (de)	stuffed.
aux Fines Herbes	with fine herbs, used of omelets etc.
Flambé(e)	flamed or flared, usually with spirit.
au Four	cooked in the oven.
Frappé(e)	chilled
Fouetté(e)	whipped, as cream.
Fumé(e)	smoked.
en Gelé(e)	jellied, as cold consommé.
Givré(e)	iced, chilled.
Glacé(e)	glazed, iced (as with icing).
en Goujons	in strips, usually fillets of fish.
au Jus	with its natural juice or gravy.
Lames de	thin slices.
Macédoine de	a mixture of fruits or vegetables, usually diced.
en Médaillons	shaped into round flat cakes.
au Naturel	with nothing added.
en Paillettes	straw-shaped.
Pané(e) à l'Anglaise	egged, breadcrumbed and deep-fried.
en Papillote	cooked in a paper bag.

sur le plat	of fried eggs.
à la Poêle	cooked in a frying pan.
au(x) Poivre(s)	cooked with peppercorns.
Rafraîchi(e)(s)	refreshed, lightly chilled.
Ramequin(s) de	cooked in ramekins (small fire-proof dishes).
Réchauffé(e)	re-heated (a branch of cookery using left-overs).
Rissolé(e)	lightly fried-over.
en Robe de Chambre	in their jackets (of potatoes).
Soufflé(e)(s)	food items that are puffed-up.
Tartelette(s) de	small open pastry cases.
en Tasse	served in a cup, usually of consommés.
en Terrine	served in a earthenware dish.
en Timbale	served in a double dish with the outside filled with ice.
sur Toast	on a slice of toast.
en Tranches	carved into slices.
en Tresses	plaited, as of fillets of fish.
Vol(s) au Vent	a large puff-pastry case filled with a savoury mixture.

Types of soup. There are seven main types of soup, each one prepared in a different fashion, as follows:

Consommé	–	A clear, meat-based soup that may be served either hot or cold as a jelly.
Purée	–	A thick soup usually prepared from pulses (peas, beans, lentils) and passed through a sieve.
Velouté	–	A soup thickened with egg yolks.
Crème	–	A thick soup made from a vegetable base and finished with cream before serving.
Bisque	–	A thick soup made from shell-fish (lobster, clams etc).
Broth	–	An unthickened soup of meat or vegetable base containing small pieces of meat, vegetables, pulses, grains etc.
Unclassified	–	This category includes such soups as oxtail, clear turtle, minestrone, and scotch broth.

4.2   COMMON FOODSTUFFS, SEASONS AND COOKING TIMES

4.2.1   TYPES OF FOODSTUFFS

In general terms, anything that is edible can be found in a restaurant of one sort or another, for some foodstuffs may be eaten in certain countries or areas and not in others, and some foodstuffs may be imported or exported and not others, depending on demand and whether they travel well or not.

In considering the situation existing in the context of the classic restaurant one is accepting, in general terms, those foodstuffs that occur naturally in Europe. To these have been added certain tropical fruits that have been encountered during various periods of colonial exploitation, such as mangoes, avocado pears etc.

The influx to Great Britain of many different ethnic groups in recent years has meant that the 'normal' list of foodstuffs available at any one time had been augmented by many others in the categories of fish, meat, vegetables and fruit.

4.2.2   SEASONS

Prior to the 1939–45 War many foods were said to be either 'in season' or 'out of season' and when 'out of season' were unobtainable either in markets, shops or restaurants.

In the case of certain fruits and vegetables 'out of season' meant that they did not grow at that time of the year in this country. They were not imported because of long transport times. In the case of fish and meats, two other factors were important, the breeding cycle, and cool storage during the summer.

Both fish and game are covered by legislation, and there are 'close seasons' when it is forbidden to hunt or catch them to protect the species.

Likewise, before refrigeration was commonplace, pork was only eaten when there was an 'r' in the month, ie September to April (the winter months), when there was less chance of it going bad.

Fresh fruit and vegetables are now available from one source or another throughout the year. Strawberries, which once only appeared on menus from late May to early July, can now be obtained during the whole year, being imported from such places as Mexico, California and Israel.

Since the advent of deep-freezing techniques, many foodstuffs are always available but not 'fresh' in the sense of being in their natural state.

4.2.2.1 Foods in season

	Jan	Feb	Mar	Apr	May	Jun	Jul	Aug	Sep	Oct	Nov	Dec
Game – Feathered												
Grouse	+							12·+	+	+	+	+20
Partridge	+	+							1+	+	+	+
Pheasant	+	+								1+	+	+
Plover								+	+	+	+	+
Ptarmigan	+	+	+	+	+	+	+	+	+	+	+	+
Quail	+	+	+	+	+	+	+	+	+	+	+	+
Snipe	+	+						+	+	+	+	+
Teal	+							+	+	+	+	+
Wild Duck	+	+						+	+	+	+	+
Woodcock	+	+							+	+	+	+
Wood Pigeon	+	+	+	+	+	+	+	+	+	+	+	+
Game – Furred												
Hare	+	+	+	+	+	+	+	+	+	+	+	+
Rabbit	+	+	+	+	+	+	+	+	+	+	+	+
Venison	+	+	+	+	Male+	+	+	+	Female+	+	+	+
Poultry												
Chicken (all sizes)	+	+	+	+	+	+	+	+	+	+	+	+
Duck	+	+	+	+	+	+	+	+	+	+	+	+
Gosling			+	+	+	+	+	+	+			
Goose								+	+	+	+	+
Guinea Fowl	+	+	+	+	+	+	+	+	+	+	+	+
Turkey	+	+	+	+	+	+	+	+	+	+	+	+

	Jan	Feb	Mar	Apr	May	Jun	Jul	Aug	Sep	Oct	Nov	Dec
Meat												
Beef	+	+	+	+	+	+	+	+	+	+	+	+
Veal	+	+	+	+	+	+	+	+	+	+	+	+
Mutton	+	+	+	+	+	+	+	+	+	+	+	+
Lamb (Home Produced)				+	+	+	+	+	+	+	+	+
Pork	+	+	+	+	+	+			+	+	+	+
Fish												
Salmon		+	+	+	+	+	+	+	+			
Salmon Trout			+	+	+	+	+	+	+			
Trout				+	+	+	+	+	+			
Mackerel				+	+	+	+	+	+	+		
Mussels	+	+	+	+					+	+	+	+
Oysters	+	+	+	+					+	+	+	+
Vegetables												
Artichokes, Globe	+	+	+	+	+	+						
Artichokes, Jerusalem	+	+	+							+	+	+
Asparagus					+	+	+	+				
Brussels Sprouts	+	+	+						+	+	+	+
Chicory	+	+	+	+						+	+	+
Vegetable Marrow							+	+	+	+		
Fruit												
Cherries						+	+	+	+			
Peaches						+	+	+	+	+	+	
Plums								+	+	+	+	+

Although many frozen foodstuffs are as good as the fresh, there are exceptions. Some soft fruits lose their firmness but are suitable for processing, eg strawberries and raspberries.

Soft fruits are usually at their best and most plentiful in high summer, June to August, but apples, pears and oranges are obtainable during most of the year from one source or another.

See table of foods in season on pp 230/231.

4.2.3 COOKING TIMES

In most restaurants offering a table d'hôte menu the majority of dishes offered are pre-prepared so as to be readily available without delay.

À la carte menus, on the other hand, by virtue of their variety must have many of their items cooked or prepared to order, which means delays, of various lengths, for diners, depending on the items chosen.

Times must be given on menus in order to inform diners of these times and to avoid possible complaints.

In general, approximate times to include cooking and service of certain typical items are as follows:

Egg dishes	up to 12 minutes
Fish dishes	10 to 20 minutes
Grilled meats (depending on size and thickness)	10 to 25 minutes
Pasta dishes	15 to 25 minutes
Roast poultry or game (depending on size)	15 to 85 minutes
Soufflés (sweet or savoury)	25 to 30 minutes

4.2.4 CUTTING OF CHEESES

Cheeses served on cheese boards or trollies should be cut as per Figure 4.11 which covers most common cheeses and shapes.

4.3 ALCOHOLIC BEVERAGES

The service of alcoholic beverages in a restaurant is probably the most profitable area to the proprietors and should be, together with the food, enjoyable to the diners.

The service of all wine should be carried out with equal respect,

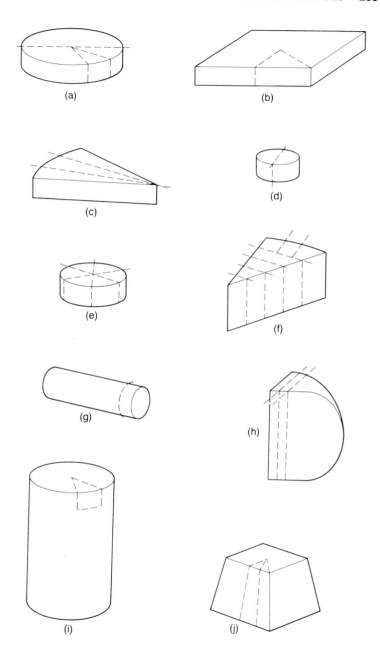

FIG. 4.11 Methods of cutting cheeses: (top to bottom) *left* – Coulommiers; Brie; Camembert; Smoked Emmental; Stilton *right* – Pont l'Eveque; Boursin; Cheddar (wedge); Edam; Fromage de Chevre

whether it be a vintage wine, or house wine. This section is only intended to be an outline of the various types, as it is not included in full in the syllabuses covered by this volume.

4.3.1 APÉRITIFS

This word means 'appetisers', and as such, means any drink which will promote an appetite, but its accepted meaning covers some items such as sherry, (qv) as well as spirits taken with vermouth and/or mixers, cocktails and those wine-based apéritifs such as Dubonnet, St Raphael and Lillet, or even, for some, fruit juices.

4.3.2 SPIRITS

These comprise those drinks composed of diluted alcohol, distilled from different vegetable materials, usually grain, each of which has its own characteristic. There are five main types, as follows:

Brandy	– Distilled from grapes, produced in several countries, but Cognac and Armagnac are from legally defined areas in France only.
Whisk(e)y	– Distilled from malted barley in the case of Scottish 'single malts', from maize in the case of the proprietary Scotch whiskies and American Bourbon and in American 'Rye'.
	Irish whiskey (with the 'e') is produced from no specified grain.
	Price differences in Scottish whiskies depend on whether they are blended or not, as well as the length of time they have been matured.
Gin	– Distilled from pure grain spirit and flavoured with juniper berries, from which the spirit gets its name (genièvre) as well as other roots and spices. Gin is probably the spirit best-suited to being drunk as an apéritif.
Rum	– A spirit distilled in various parts of the West Indies from sugar-cane and/or molasses.
	Rum varies from the clear Bacardi and golden Jamaican to brown Demerara.
Vodka	– A clear spirit originating in Russia and Poland and distilled either from grain or potatoes.
Other types	– Various other spirits are produced in different countries, such as the German Schnapps and Korn; Danish Akvavit, Greek Ouzo, Mexican Tequila,

and several based on fruit, such as Slivovitz (Yugoslavia), Calvados (Normandy), and the Swiss and Alsatian Eaux de Vie made from cherries, as well as those made from raspberries, strawberries, plums and pears.

4.3.3. FORTIFIED WINES

The term 'fortified wines' means those wines which have brandy added to them, and embraces sherry, port, madeira and marsala, as well as vermouths and those wine-based apéritifs mentioned in section 4.3.1.

Sherry
— Only produced in South-West Spain, although it is copied in several other countries. All sherries are blended, using the so-called 'Solera' system, which keeps the quality and character constant. Sherry types run from the very driest (Fino) through Amontillado, Manzanilla, Oloroso and Cream to Brown, and one can generalise by saying that the lighter colour a sherry is the drier it will be.

Port
— Produced only in Portugal around the valley of the river Douro, it is shipped from the town of Oporto, from whence it gets its name.
Port comes in three colours, Ruby, White, and Tawny. Ruby is the youngest, and therefore the cheapest. White is made from white grapes only, and can be either sweet or dry. Tawny is usually older than ruby, and is matured in cask until it becomes tawny. This can take from 7 to 30 years.
Vintage Ports are those made in years when the shippers 'declare a vintage.' All vintage ports are blends of the same year, and will be matured from 10 to 30 years.

Madeira
— Produced on the Atlantic island of the same name, madeira wines are all blended, being made under the 'Solera' system, as is sherry.
There are four main styles, each of which has its own character and traditional usage: Sercial (light amber – for apéritifs); Verdelho (rich golden – before or after meals); Bual or Boal (a sweet dessert wine); Malmsey (dark and rich – a good substitute for port at the end of a meal).

Marsala   – A fortified wine coming from the island of Sicily. A good dessert wine with uses in the kitchen for sauces and dessert dishes.

Vermouths   – These are made from wines blended together, flavoured with herbs (some 40–50) including worm-wood (Vermut (Ger)) from which the drink gets its name. The majority come from Italy, and can be sweet or dry, and red, white or rose. Vermouths are both fortified wines and apéritifs in their own right.

4.3.4 BEVERAGE WINES

Beverage wines are the fermented juice of the grape, and are produced in many countries of the world, the most notable of which are France, Italy, Spain and Germany.

Wine is either still or sparkling, and can be either red, white or rosé, and the classic wines are usually bottled in easily recognisable bottles, most of which denote their origin, as shown in Figure 4.12.

By tradition, each type of wine also has its own shape of glass, and where possible, these should be kept to, but failing the complete range, standard glasses for serving red and white wines should be available (see section 2.2.4).

FIG. 4.12 Standard Bottle Shape (l. to r.) Bordeaux, Red; White; Burgundy, Red; Sparkling, Champagne; Rose d'Anjou; Moselle; Hock

4.3.5 BEERS, LAGERS AND CIDERS

Beers and lagers are made from an infusion of malted barley and water, flavoured with hops and allowed to ferment.

The different character of beers is due to several factors, not least being the degree of roasting of the malt, the type of hops used, and the origin and mineral content of the water.

The types of beers usually offered for sale are ales, stouts/porters, and lagers.

Ales — Can be either light or brown in colour, and mild or bitter in flavour.

Stout/Porter — Full in character and very dark in colour (almost black), the best-known being Guinness.

Lagers — A very light type of beer originating in Germany and Czechoslovakia, although two Danish lagers are world-famous, Tuborg and Carlsberg.

The character of beers in general varies from place to place depending on local tastes.

Cider and Perry — These are made from the fermented juice of apples and pears respectively. They vary from very sweet to very dry and a whole range is made. Some ciders and perries are made sparkling, and are sold in the same bottle-dress as champagnes, marketed as Pomagne.

4.3.6 LIQUEURS

As their names imply, several of the many liqueurs on sale have their origins in the monastic houses of Europe, where they originated as medicaments, notably as digestives, and this has continued to the present-day. They are drunk normally at the end of a meal, although some are used as constituents of cocktails.

There are well over 70 of them, and they are of varying alcoholic strength. They are mainly either herb and spice-based, or fruit-based, although a few are based on coffee or chocolate.

4.4 RESTAURANT BILLING

Waiter's billing systems, if operated correctly, fulfil three main functions, as follows:

Supply — They are a means of obtaining goods from the kitchen, bar, etc for supply to customers.

Record – When summarised, they are thus a means of recording sales of individual items of 'stock'.

Revenue – By ensuring that each item issued is charged to the customer, or otherwise officially accounted for, turnover figures are produced, and control on possible fraudulent practices carried out.

There are many systems in operation, some simple, other more complicated, but all must have the means of carrying out these three functions. An 8-total cash register is shown in Figure 4.13, which will supply 8 separate totals of analysis of sales, headings can be chosen, as needed. Systems can vary from hand-written to computer-operated, and the adoption of any particular one is a matter of management decision, based usually, on the type of restaurant operation to be used.

The most usual one operated in a first-class restaurant is known as the 'Continental' or triplicate checking system. This consists of an order pad interleaved with double-sided carbon paper, each

FIG. 4.13 An 8-total electronic Cash Register (Norfrond)

order consisting of a top-copy, a bottom copy, and a centre copy which alone is made from a translucent paper, enabling it to be read easily, though the carbon image is made on its reverse side.

The top copy is destined for kitchen or bar, and is the original, the bottom copy (carbon) going to the cashier. The flimsy copy is kept by the waiter at his sideboard, as an 'aide-mémoire'.

The cashier has responsibility for charging all items on each check and the kitchen for issuing only those items written, with no later alterations made, or permitted.

Any further issues made due to accident, customer dislike, or other valid reason (such as complimentaries) must be made on a check counter-signed by either head waiter or restaurant manager. Other systems which are based on total waiter-responsibility are those with tear-off strips filled in by the waiter as kitchen checks, and these should be priced on the bills made out by the waiter himself. Should the control office find checks have been issued and not charged, then the waiter bears financial responsibility for subsequent payment.

Another system is used on the continent, mainly in brasserie-type operations. Waiters use a multi-operator register, each waiter having his own key, and therefore his own total. Waiters will 'ring-up' items required, a check is issued, serving as a kitchen check;

FIG. 4.14 A computerised restaurant billing machine (Retail Control Systems Ltd)

the waiter will collect goods, collect the payment from the diners, and at the end of the day the register is read, and the waiter then pays in the amount recorded against his key.

Newer developments used more in popular catering outlets are computerised systems in which the waiter keys in the items ordered, the machine having a numbered button for each menu item. A printer situated in the kitchen will then print out the order. A machine of this type is shown in Figure 4.14.

All debits are stored in memory until the waiter requires the diner's bill when it is printed out complete, and on settlement, that transaction is cleared. All items sold are recorded cumulatively, so that management reports on stock levels, as well as revenue, can be obtained, at any time.

Many of these machines also have a staff-recording function which is very useful in operations open for 18–24 hours and employing either casual or full-time staff, who 'clock-on' and 'off', using the register, which also works-out gross or net time on duty in order to calculate wage payments due.

Even in those establishments operating the 'continental' or triplicate system, many cashiers and bars are now supplied with key-pads and terminals connected to hotel computer systems, in order that restaurant charges may be entered directly on to diners' hotel bills.

4.5   BASIC LEGAL ASPECTS – OUTLINE

As there are many books already covering this subject fully, and in view of the differing legal situation between England, Wales and Scotland it is our intention only to include those areas which directly involve waiting staff as agents of their employers with regard to service of food and drink, and with their general dealings with guests.

4.5.1   SERVICE OF ALCOHOLIC BEVERAGES

Permitted age for general consumption of alcoholic beverages is 18 years. However, those over 16 may be supplied with beer, porter, cider or perry to accompany a meal.

No person under the age of 18 can be allowed to dispense alcoholic beverages, nor be concerned with their direct service.

4.5.2 LICENSING OR PERMITTED HOURS

'Permitted hours' or those times when alcoholic beverages may be served to members of the public vary throughout the United Kingdom, and as local licensing justices have powers to vary these times waiting staff must make themselves aware of the times applicable to their own establishments, and also to the legal position regarding 'drinking-up time'.

4.5.3 WEIGHTS AND MEASURES

Beers, lagers and ciders unless pre-packed (ie bottled or canned) must be sold in multiples of half-pints in Government stamped glasses.

Spirits, viz whisky, gin, rum and vodka must be sold only in quantities of $\frac{1}{4}$, $\frac{1}{5}$ or $\frac{1}{6}$ of a gill or multiples thereof, and the measure employed in a particular bar must be displayed in that bar and on wine lists (see Weights and Measures Act, 1963).

Wine may be sold by the 'glass' in unstamped glasses. However, legislation is being changed to permit sales of open wines only in stamped glasses, or if in a carafe, by fixed measures (see Weights and Measures (Sale of Wine) Order 1976).

4.5.4 MENU DESCRIPTION

Waiters must be aware that it is an offence under the Trade Descriptions Act, 1968 to describe a menu item falsely, eg 'buttered carrots', must be coated in butter and not in margarine.

4.5.5 PRICING OF MENUS

All prices on the menus must include VAT and a priced menu must be displayed outside the restaurant. Service charge, if levied as a percentage, must be clearly stated, under the terms of the Price Marking (Food & Drink on the Premises) Order 1979.

4.5.6 LIABILITY FOR GUESTS' PROPERTY

If the waiter accepts guests' property eg coats, wraps, cameras, for safekeeping while the guests have their meal, then they technically accept liability for those items on behalf of the proprietor. A waiter should, therefore, fully acquaint himself with the policy and practice of his establishment in respect to handling guests' property.

4.6 HEALTH AND SAFETY

Under the dual headings of both the Health and Safety at Work Act 1974, and common sense, the waiting staff must be always vigilant in trying to avoid accidents which will affect them, their colleagues, and their customers.

Each establishment will have its own house rules or guide lines laid down for safety procedures to be adopted. The following notes will assist in determining safety procedures.

4.6.1 ACCIDENT PREVENTION AND REPORTING

4.6.1.1 Diners

Some of the common accidents involving diners are as follows:
Waiter spills something on a diner:

> Waiter should apologise for the mishap.
> Offer a damp serviette for diner to mop up spill himself.

Inform head waiter/restaurant manager who will take further necessary steps (eg enter incident in incident book; take diner's name and address; offer to pay for cleaning garment/s) and generally try to placate the diner.
Spillage caused by diner himself:

> Waiter should reassure the diner that all can be put right.
> Offer damp serviette/s, for diner to mop up spill himself.
> Move diners to another table, if necessary.
> Re-serve the meal, if necessary.
> Report to head-waiter/restaurant manager, as above.

Any other accidents requiring first-aid must be reported immediately to head waiter/restaurant manager who will take necessary action.

4.6.1.2 Staff

A waiter should cultivate safe working practices at all times to minimise the risk of accidents, eg use of correct doors to enter/leave the service area, no running in the restaurant or service area.

Immediate cleansing to be undertaken of any spillages; broken glass to be safely disposed of in special receptacles provided. All ashtrays to be emptied at the end of each service into metal bins provided to avoid fire risk.

All accidents involving members of staff should be reported to the head waiter or restaurant manager.

4.6.2   *EMERGENCIES, BOMB ALERTS*

Most establishments have their own procedures laid down for the above situations, which must be rigidly adhered to. However, staff must always be vigilant and report any suspicious packages, persons, etc, to the head waiter/restaurant manager.

4.6.3   *FIRE PROCEDURES*

Fire procedures will be laid down by management in consultation with the local Fire Prevention Officer.

Contents of all procedural notices must be strictly adhered to, but waiting staff must take care to see that all fire or emergency exits are kept free of any obstacles and unlocked at all times that the premises are occupied.

4.6.4   *LOST PROPERTY*

Guests may inadvertently leave personal property in the restaurant, such as coats, wraps, hats, cigarettes and lighters, handbags, cameras, etc.

Procedure for dealing with items found will often be covered by house rules, but as a general principle any items found after the diners have left, should be handed over to the head waiter or restaurant manager, who should record the item together with the date, table number, name of the guest, if known, and the name of the finder. On no account should the waiter keep the item himself.

4.6.5   *HYGIENE*

Under current food hygiene legislation, the Environmental Health Officers are empowered to enter any catering establishment in order to inspect the premises and practices carried out therein, with powers of immediate closure for infringements of the Acts. It is therefore in the best interests of all employees to cultivate hygienic working practices, and take reasonable care to protect all food from contamination while it is in their care.

Lack of hygiene may cause an outbreak of food poisoning resulting in adverse publicity and consequent loss of custom for the establishment.

In the order to minimise the risk, the waiting staff should observe the following main points with regard to themselves, their equipment, and the food that they handle.

4.6.5.1 Self and habits

Hair. Must be clean and well-groomed. Long hair must be tied back, and not combed or handled in the restaurant.

Teeth and oral hygiene. Bad breath offends and carries germs. Counter this by regular brushing of teeth and visits to the dentist. Eating of strongly flavoured foods (eg garlic), or smoking, before service should be avoided.

Hands and fingernails. Hands should be kept clean without nicotine stains, and fingernails short, well scrubbed and not bitten. Hands should be washed after using the toilet. No coloured nail-varnish should be worn.

Body-cleanliness. Regular bathing or showering is a must for all waiting staff. Deodorants and foot powders should be used if necessary, but should not be highly scented.

Clothing. Should be kept clean at all times, with daily changes of socks or stockings, and underclothing.

Nose, mouth, hair and forehead. Should not be handled during the service.

Waiter's cloth. Should on no account be used as a handkerchief or duster, nor should it be carried on the shoulder, under the arm, or in the pocket.

Coughing or sneezing. Should be done into a handkerchief and the hands washed after each occasion.

Smoking. Illegal in all food preparation areas and behind bars.

Cuts, burns and sores. Must be covered with waterproof dressings.

Illnesses. All cases of illness, in particular, diarrhoea, must be reported to the head waiter in the first instance, and a doctor consulted.

4.6.5.2 Equipment

Service spoons and forks, tea and coffee spoons. Must be immaculately clean and not washed in a jug of hot water on the sideboard.

Other service equipment.   Cheeseboards, carving trollies etc. must be kept scrupulously clean.

Glasses, cups.   Should not be used if chipped or cracked.

Crockery.   Stained or caked crockery must be returned to the wash-up for re-washing (by hand if necessary).

4.6.5.3   Food

Many foods are susceptible to growth of harmful bacteria in certain conditions, and care must be taken to avoid this.

As a general rule, hot food must be kept hot, and cold food refrigerated until just before the service begins.

All food should be returned to the kitchen immediately it has been served, and any food presented on cold counters, trollies, etc, must be returned to the kitchen at the end of the lunch service, and not left out until dinner.

Care must be taken to avoid flies in the restaurant, and any food on show must be adequately protected against them, and in the case of self-service counters, sneeze-guards should be fitted to glass screens.

Food should *never* be handled with bare hands.

4.7   HANDLING CUSTOMER COMPLAINTS

Despite best efforts from waiting staff, complaints of one sort or another are inevitable.

They are usually centred around four distinct areas, viz: Food; Service; Staff; Facilities.

4.7.1   FOOD

The complaints about food may relate to hot food being cold, size of portion, degree of cooking, quality of food etc. The responsibility for these lies with the chef.

So far as possible, the waiter should make every effort to handle the complaint himself, have the food re-heated, and then inform his head waiter, who may decide to take any further action necessary.

Should the complaint be of a nature beyond the scope of the waiter, eg size of portion etc, then the head waiter should be informed immediately.

4.7.2   SERVICE

Complaints about service can be either about quality of service or speed of service.

A complaint about delay in service, if due to the kitchen, should be referred to the head waiter immediately. Where delay in service can be anticipated due to any other circumstances, a waiter should tactfully inform the diners of a possible delay, which may avoid a complaint later, as some diners may be in more of a hurry than others.

4.7.3   STAFF

Complaints about behaviour or attitude of staff will normally be made either verbally to the head waiter, or in writing to the management. It is therefore in the interest of all waiting staff to develop a manner in dealing with customers which will not cause offence in any way (refer to section 2.1.2, 'Social skills').

4.7.4   FACILITIES

Most complaints about facilities will relate to the state of or provisions in the toilet facilities, and any such complaints should be directed to the head waiter for immediate action.

4.8   MODES OF ADDRESS

In the restaurant or banqueting context it will often be necessary to address titled guests, on their reception, or at table, in which case the proper form must be used. This will vary according to their rank, or in the case of academic or clerical titles, their degree, or office held.

The title itself will normally only be used on place cards or by a Master of Ceremonies, on introducing the guests, in a formal banqueting situation.

Title	Mode of Address
Royalty	
H M The Queen	Your Majesty *then* Ma'am
H M The Queen Mother	Your Majesty *then* Ma'am

Duke of Edinburgh Princes, Princesses Dukes & Duchesses of Royal Blood	Your Royal Highness *then* Sir or Madam

Peerage

Dukes & Duchesses	Your Grace
Marquess & Marchioness	Lord or Lady . . .
Earls & Countesses	Lord or Lady . . .
Viscounts & Viscountesses	Lord or Lady . . .
Barons & Baronesses	Lord or Lady . . .
Baronet	Sir (*Christian name*)
Baronet's wife	Lady (*Surname*)
Knight & wife	as for Baronet & wife
Dame	Dame (*Christian name*)

Government Service

Ambassadors	Your Excellency or Sir
High Commissioners	Your Excellency or Sir
Cabinet Minister	Minister/Sir or Madam
Privy Councillor	Minister/Sir or Madam

Clerical

The Pope	Your Holiness
Archbishop	Your Grace
Bishop	My Lord or Your Lordship
Dean	Mr Dean
Canon	Canon . . .
Vicar/Rector	Vicar or Rector or Mr . . .
Catholic Priest	Father . . .
Rabbi	Rabbi . . .

Service

Rank	Rank . . . or Sir
e.g. Admiral	Admiral . . . or Sir

Civil

Lord Chief Justice	If a Peer, address accordingly otherwise My Lord or Your Lordship
High Court Judge	My Lord or Your Lordship
County or Crown Court Judges	Judge or Judge . . . or Sir
Aldermen	Mr Alderman or Mrs Alderman
Lord Mayors & Lady Mayoresses	My Lord/My Lady or Mr Mayor or Your Worship

Councillor	Councillor . . . or Sir or Madam
Citizen	Sir or Mr . . .
Citizen's wife	Madam . . . or Mrs . . .
Citizen's son (young)	Master . . . (*with Christian name or Surname*)
Citizen's daughter	Miss . . .
Academic	
Professor	Professor . . .
Doctor	Doctor . . .

REVISION QUESTIONS

CHAPTER 1

1. What are the main obligations of an inn?
2. Define an 'ordinary'.
3. What is the origin of the term 'restaurant'?
4. What was the social effect that the formation of tea-shops brought about?
5. A recent introduction in hotels is the coffee shop. How does this differ from the 'classic restaurant'?
6. Consider the features necessary in a restaurant. State five of them.
7. What facilities must be provided in a restaurant, by law?
8. Which factors will determine the type of tables and seating to be provided in a restaurant?
9. Name the ancillary departments under the control of the restaurant manager.
10. Under whose control is the hotplate area?
11. Why are cold items collected before hot in the kitchen?
12. Name the items supplied to the restaurant by the still-room.
13. What is the purpose of a burnishing machine?
14. State the purpose and mode of use of a 'Polivit' plate.
15. How should spare stock of crockery be stored?
16. Define the purpose of a restaurant pantry.
17. Why should glasses not be washed in a dishwasher?
18. What is the purpose of the Dispense Bar?
19. What equipment should the Dispense Bar contain?
20. What is the general principle operated by Linen Rooms for issues?
21. State the main functions of the Control Office.
22. Name the two main types of service operated in popular catering and fast-food operations.
23. In self-service operations, why are different counter configurations used?

24. State the five main types of service used in restaurants, explaining the difference between them.

25. Describe the operation of the classic French 'Brigade de Restaurant'.

26. What is the function of the 'chef de rang'?

27. What is the function of the 'sommelier'?

28. State three functions performed by waiting-staff uniforms.

CHAPTER 2

1. What three qualities must a waiter possess?

2. Which physical quality must a waiter have?

3. Why is personal hygiene so important for waiting staff?

4. Discuss briefly the reasons for smart appearance in waiting staff.

5. State the reasons for having legible handwriting in waiting staff.

6. Waiting staff should always arrive punctually on duty. Discuss.

7. Why should a waiter have a good memory? Discuss.

8. State the three moral qualities necessary for waiting staff.

9. Should waiting staff have good speech habits? Discuss.

10. A waiter should give 'service without servility'. Discuss.

11. Why is good menu knowledge necessary for waiting staff?

12. Discuss the waiter/guest relationship.

13. State two reasons for the popularity of round tables in restaurants

14. What diameter table should be used to accommodate 10 persons?

15. What is the use of an 'allonge'?

16. What is the biggest disadvantage of 'banquette' seating?

17. Why should chair-backs be narrower at the top than at the base?

18. State the main features necessary for sideboards or 'dumb-waiters'.

19. List cutlery in general use in restaurants.

20. List the sizes of plates used in restaurants and state the purpose for which they are used.

21. State the categories of glasses used in restaurants.

22. Name eight pieces of cutlery which are used for the service of special dishes.

23. What size tablecloth will be needed for a table of size 3×3 ft (914×914 mm)?

24. Why is pure linen used for the manufacture of glass cloths?

25. List ten different types of trolley used in restaurants.

26. When not involved in other tasks, a waiter should stand by his side-board, facing into the restaurant'. What is the reason for this statement?

27. What size of tray should be used in transporting items from kitchen to restaurant?

28. Why should sideboard tops be kept clear?

29. Which methods of carrying empty glasses should be employed in the following circumstances:– (i) during mise-en-place period;
     (ii) with diners in the restaurant;
     (iii) after the service?

30. What items are usually served with a spoon only?

31. What cutlery is suitable for the service of most food items?

32. Which items of food are best served using two fish knives?

33. Which items of food are best served with one fork?

34. Give two examples of foods that can be served with two forks.

35. A well-decorated dish has been brought from the kitchen. What should the waiter do before serving?

36. 'If serving from an hors-d'oeuvre or other trolley it is best to stand behind it.' Give the reason for this statement.

37. Why might washed cutlery need a final polish before use? Give two reasons.

38. Why must all glasses be checked for absolute cleanliness?

39. What would your first action be if crockery washed by machine came out clean, but with water spots on?

40. State three uses for a waiter's cloth.

41. Why is correct posture necessary when serving at table.

42. What precaution would you take before serving food to a diner?

43. If 'badged' crockery is used, how should it be placed on the table?

44. Describe how food should be arranged on a diner's plate.

45. Before clearing between courses, what sign would you look for to indicate that diners had finished eating?

46. What action would be carried out after clearing the main course and before the sweet course is served?

47. Describe the method of changing ashtrays at table, and state the reasons.

CHAPTER 3

1. How should polished wood furniture be maintained: (i) In normal use; (ii) If greasy from handling?

2. What treatment would be used to clean a Formica or other plastic finish?

3. What procedure would you adopt to ensure quickest, most efficient cleaning of a carpeted floor, before the service?

4. What procedure would you adopt to clean a carpeted floor, if food has been spilt onto it?

5. State the two methods possible to clean thermo-plastic tiles.

6. What method of cleaning would be adopted for walls covered with flock wallpapers or hessian?

7. In restaurants having heavy drapes, what maintenance must be carried out between cleaning?

8. What is the most important principle to be adopted when carrying furniture?

9. What two factors should be considered in allowing space between tables in laying out the restaurant?

10. How should trollies be manoeuvred: (i) in normal use, and (ii) in negotiating doorways?

11. State the three main reasons that table-cloths are used in restaurants.

12. What two items could be used to steady a rocking table?

13. What should be looked for in the centre crease of a banqueting table-cloth?

14. Name the cutlery required to lay-up a cover for a three-course meal.

15. What items will an à la carte cover consist of?

16. Give two reasons against using ornately-folded serviettes.

17. Why should the contents of cruets be checked daily?

18. What happens to English mustard prepared from powder if it is not discarded after each service?

19. Suggest a standard lay-out for a restaurant sideboard.

20. What action should be taken after cleaning flare lamps?

21. What maintenance of proprietary sauce bottles is required?

22. Describe the preparation of 'Melba Toast'.

23. State the four usual methods of presenting butter in a high-class restaurant.

24. Why should water jugs be placed on linen serviettes on service plates or salvers?

25. Name three dishes which require finger bowls to be served.

26. How should cut lemon be stored to prevent drying out?

27. If laying a table with two glasses, one for red and one for white wine, where should they be placed, and why?

28. Why should large flower vases not be used on restaurant tables?

29. Why should the water in flower vases be frequently changed?

30. State in one word the impression that should be given to intending diners.

31. List the actions that should be carried out as soon as guests arrive at your table/station.

32. Why is it important to recognise the 'host' of a party of diners?

33. Ideally, how many menus should be presented at a table?

34. For which courses initially should the diners' order be taken?

35. How should the waiter's check be written out?

36. Define the following: (i) a 'Retour' check; (ii) a 'Retour/en place' check; (iii) 'Supplement'; (iv) 'Suite'.

37. What facts should a sommelier know before approaching a table to take a wine order?

38. Why should petrol-filled cigarette lighters not be used by waiters?

39. List one factor that must be taken into account when dealing with each of the following groups of customers: (i) Babies; (ii) Children; (iii) Handicapped persons.

40. How many services of butter should be used for a party of 12 covers?

41. When should water be served at a table?

42. What task should be carried out between taking the order and serving the first course?

43. State the presentation and accompaniment for a fruit cocktail.

44. State the accompaniment for melon.

45. Give the cover and accompaniment for an hors-d'oeuvre varié.

46. Describe the service of a standard soup.

47. Describe the cover and service for a consommé.

48. State the adjuncts for soupe à l'oignon.

49. What is the most common adjunct for all pasta or farinaceous dishes?

50. What type of egg dishes are not normally served at lunch or dinner?

51. What cover would be required for the service of Omelette Arnold Bennett?

52. State the cover and accompaniments for Moules à la Marinière.

53. Why are two sizes of plate possible on which to serve fish?

54. What type of knife should be served for use with steaks?

55. List the accompaniments for Boeuf rôti à l'Anglaise.

56. Give the two possible sauces to be served with cold asparagus.

57. State the possible methods of serving side salads.

58. What is the cover and what accompaniments are usually served with savouries?

59. When should cheese be served during a meal? State two alternatives.

60. Describe the presentation and cover for the service of fresh fruit.

61. Which sauce is that usually served with braised ham or tongue?

62. From what is mayonnaise composed?

63. Which proprietary sauces are usually kept in a first-class restaurant?

64. State the rule regarding the temperature at which wine should be served.

65. What should guests be asked if they have ordered spirits with mixers?

66. Define 'Russian' tea and describe its service.

67. Describe the service of China tea.

68. What is a 'tisane'?

69. Which type of coffee is the only one to be boiled in its preparation?

70. Other than tea or coffee, list the other beverages that are obtained from the Still-Room.

71. State the difference between mineral waters and table waters.

72. State the uses of a slip-cloth.

73. Having been asked for the bill by a diner, what three things should a waiter do?

74. What 8 methods of settling a guest's bill are possible?

75. If a bill is spoiled, what procedure should be adopted?

76. What type of cleaning should be carried out between lunch and dinner?

77. What operation is often carried out by restaurant staff before leaving at night?

CHAPTER 4

1. State the difference between an à la carte and table d'hôte menu.

2. State the two types of breakfast and describe each.

3. Describe briefly the differences between the foods served at luncheon and dinner.

4. State the difference between afternoon tea and high tea.

5. Define supper as a meal.

6. Which two 'questions' should be answered by a menu?

7. Describe the term 'sauté'.

8. State in French and English the four terms used to denote degree of cooking steaks.

9. Define a 'cromesqui'.

10. Define the six main classifications of soups.

11. What are the two main reasons for foods being either in or out of season.

12. Why is it necessary to include cooking times of certain items on à la carte menus?

13. What is the accepted definition of the term aperitifs?

14. Name the five main types of spirits used in bars.

15. Define the term 'fortified wines'. List the main types.

16. Define briefly what is meant by beverage wines.

17. State the types and colours of beverage wines.

18. Name the main types of beers and state the differences between them.

19. Define the term liqueurs and state their use.

20. What are the three main functions of waiter's billing systems?

21. What is the name of the system of billing usually adopted in first-class restaurants?

22. State the purpose and destination of each of the parts of a waiter's check.

23. Which alcoholic beverages may be supplied to those persons over 16 years and under 18 years old?

24. What is the meaning of the term 'permitted hours'?

25. Which four spirits are specified by the notice which must be displayed in bars under the terms of the Weights and Measures Act 1963?

26. Which legislation makes it illegal to falsely describe menu items?

27. What condition is placed on restaurant operators under the terms of the Price Marking (Food and Drink on the Premises) Order 1979?

28. What is the legal situation if a waiter takes a guest's coat to hang up for the guest?

29. What should a waiter do if he spills some food onto a guest?

30. What type of behaviour is expected from staff under the terms of the Health and Safety at Work Act 1974?

31. What procedures should be adopted regarding lost or found property is a restaurant?

32. What should never be used to handle food?

33. State the four main areas of possible complaint in a restaurant.

34. If in a junior position, to whom would you refer any complaints made to you?

INDEX